THE BOY WHO BECAME

BUFFALO BILL

GROWING UP BILLY CODY IN BLEEDING KANSAS

THE BOY WHO BECAME
BUFFALO BILL

GROWING UP BILLY CODY IN BLEEDING KANSAS

ANDREA WARREN

two lions

Published by Two Lions, New York

www.apub.com

Amazon, the Amazon logo, and Two Lions are trademarks of Amazon.com, Inc.,
or its affiliates.

ISBN 978-1-4778-2718-5 (hardcover)

ISBN 978-1-4778-2871-7 (paperback)

ISBN 978-1-4778-7716-6 (digital)

Book design by Ryan Michaels

Printed in the United States of America

FIRST EDITION

10 9 8 7 6 5 4 3 2 1

For my siblings—
Jim Warren, Steve Warren,
Mary Warren, and Debi Warren Fast—
with love and gratitude.

TABLE OF
CONTENTS

A NOTE OF CAUTION TO READERS VIII

USE OF TERMINOLOGY IN THIS BOOK IX

PROLOGUE, 1894 XI

CHAPTER 1   LOSING SAM 1

CHAPTER 2   ON THE ROAD TO KANSAS 7

CHAPTER 3   SLAVERY BECOMES REAL....................... 12

CHAPTER 4   BILLY VISITS FORT LEAVENWORTH........17

CHAPTER 5   ARRIVING IN THE PROMISED LAND........23

CHAPTER 6   AT HOME IN THE VALLEY.......................32

CHAPTER 7   ISAAC CODY'S BLOODY TRAIL 40

CHAPTER 8   PRO-SLAVE OR FREE STATE? 48

CHAPTER 9   BILLY SOUNDS THE ALARM....................56

CHAPTER 10   BILLY MEETS THE ABOLITIONISTS.........66

CHAPTER 11   JOHN BROWN'S WAR IN KANSAS 73

CHAPTER 12   FATHER 79

CHAPTER 13   BILLY THE HERO 86

CHAPTER 14   TROUBLE WITH THE MORMONS..............94

CHAPTER 15   BILLY AND THE INDIANS 105

CHAPTER 16   BILLY RIDES THE PONY EXPRESS.........114

CHAPTER 17   BILLY'S VOLUNTEER WAR 123

CHAPTER 18   BILLY JOINS THE RED LEGS 129

CHAPTER 19   QUANTRILL TAKES REVENGE.................134

CHAPTER 20   MOTHER 143

CHAPTER 21   PRIVATE CODY: SCOUT AND SPY 147

CHAPTER 22   A SOLDIER'S LIFE................................155

CHAPTER 23   BECOMING BUFFALO BILL 161

CHAPTER 24   BUFFALO BILL'S WILD WEST 170

THE LATER LIFE AND LEGACY OF THE BOY FROM

             BLEEDING KANSAS...................................187

AUTHOR'S NOTE...207

ACKNOWLEDGMENTS 211

MORE ABOUT BUFFALO BILL AND HIS TIMES 213

NOTES 220

BIBLIOGRAPHY 230

PICTURE CREDITS 232

INDEX..233

A NOTE OF CAUTION
TO READERS

Buffalo Bill Cody was a master at telling compelling stories that enthralled his listeners, but he struggled to remember dates, places, and sometimes facts. He wrote his autobiography three different times. It's possible that his press agent embellished some of the stories in the last two. I constructed Cody's childhood based on his written accounts and those of his sisters, in concordance with most—but not all—of Cody's historians. I have verified whatever information I could and have chosen to leave out reported incidents in his life that seemed highly improbable.

F TERMINOLOGY
N THIS BOOK

◆·◆

[N]ative American"? "Native"? "Indigenous
["]Indian"? Which term is correct? I thought
[ ]" until I toured the Smithsonian's splendid
[ ]e American Indian in Washington, DC. My
[ ]aho tribe, used the word "Indian" to refer to
[ ]that we observed around us. So I asked him
[ ]said that we are welcome to use the term
[ ]comfortable with "Indian." The museum's
[t]he terms above are acceptable.

I have used a mix of terms in this book, picking whichever one
felt the most appropriate at the moment. Wherever possible, I have
used specific tribal names, and when I have used the word "Indian,"
I have done so with the greatest respect.

IX

Rosa Bonheur
— 1889 —

PROLOGUE

1894

❖ ◆ ❖

A thundering cheer rose through the grandstand the moment the crowd caught sight of Buffalo Bill entering the arena. There he was, tall and ramrod straight on his splendid horse. He was dressed in light buckskin and wore fine leather boots and a Stetson hat. Long hair and a neatly trimmed goatee framed his handsome face. He rode around the arena, doffing his hat to his delighted audience. Never had there been a more magnificent Western man!

Behind him came the enormous cast of his Wild West extravaganza—seven hundred people in all. They included the famed sharpshooter Annie Oakley; cowboys and cowgirls; more than two

---

OPPOSITE: Of the many paintings of him, this was Buffalo Bill Cody's favorite. The French artist Rosa Bonheur created the original in 1889, and it was slightly altered at a later date.

hundred Native American men, women, and children all dressed in their ceremonial finest; and colorfully costumed riders from all over the world—Russian Cossacks, South American gauchos, Mexican vaqueros, and English lancers. There was even a brass band, and animals, too, including buffalo, burros, Texas steers, bears, elk, and hundreds of horses, all coming together in a grand show that had thrilled audiences all over the world.

But it was Buffalo Bill everyone came to see. They couldn't get enough of him. They eagerly read the show's program notes telling how he had ridden the Pony Express at age fourteen, worked as a scout and a guide for the army, fought in the Civil War, and then become a legendary buffalo hunter and a heroic Indian fighter. For the latter he had received the Congressional Medal of Honor. He'd counted several American presidents as friends, and his legion of admirers included everyone from the American writer Mark Twain to the British statesman Winston Churchill, and even Queen Victoria herself.

But there was so much more to him than his public persona. His audiences knew little about his boyhood along the violent Kansas-Missouri border in the bloody years preceding the Civil War, when he was known as Billy Cody. The program notes did not mention the grief he carried all his life for his older brother, who had died when Billy was a child, or the fear he had felt when his father was a hunted man. They knew little about the dangers he and his family had experienced for many years, the hardships they had endured, and their perpetual worries over money. People read about his exciting adventures, but not the responsibilities he took on after his father's death, leaving him at age eleven to support and protect his family.

Had they known all this, they would have understood how growing up in Bleeding Kansas in those years before the Civil War had shaped him, and how that experience had propelled him and prepared him for what he was to become: the world's greatest showman and the embodiment of the American West in its glory days.

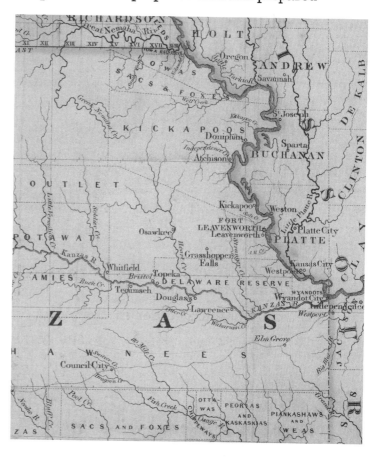

Kansas was originally known as Kanzas, a word that came from the native Kanza Indians, and one that is used on this 1855 map. Note the Missouri River, forming the boundary between northeastern Kansas and Missouri.

CHAPTER 1

LOSING SAM

—◆•◆—

Billy Cody was with his brother when the accident happened. It was a bright, crisp September day in 1853, and the boys were on horseback, going out to round up the cows near the family's Iowa farm. Seven-year-old Billy was on his pony, and twelve-year-old Sam rode Betsy—even though Mother had warned him just that morning to stay away from the high-strung mare. She's much too skittish, Mother had told him. And much too dangerous.

But Sam paid no attention, for hadn't he always been able to manage any horse? Billy idolized his strong, handsome big brother. He wasn't worried about Betsy, because Sam could do anything!

At first Betsy behaved, moving along at an easy trot. But suddenly she bucked wildly, trying to throw Sam. She stomped and snorted, jerking her head to and fro and lunging hard. Sam hung on tight, grinning at his little brother to show that he wasn't afraid.

Then the unthinkable happened. In an instant, Betsy reared up on her hind legs. Billy watched helplessly as his brother frantically tried to rein her in, but the horse was completely out of control. In panicked frenzy, she lost all sense of balance and came crashing

Frontier life could be full of danger for both adults and children, and Sam's accident was not unusual.

backward, hitting the ground with a terrible thud, crushing Sam beneath her.

As Betsy struggled to her feet and began to trot away, Billy rushed to his unconscious brother. A neighbor who saw the accident came running to help. He offered to carry Sam to his house and send for the doctor. He told Billy to get his father as fast as he could.

Billy sped off, his heart pounding. He knew that his father was at a political meeting not far away and quickly found him. Isaac Cody calmed Billy enough to find out what had happened, then took Billy's pony and raced to the neighbor's home. Billy followed on foot, running as fast as he could. When he got there, his parents and five sisters

were already at Sam's side. One glance at his mother's face confirmed Billy's worst fears.

The doctor worked all night to save Sam, but he died before
daylight.

Billy crumpled under the weight of his grief. His best friend,
his playmate, the big brother he looked up to and loved so much,
was gone. The day of the funeral he slipped away to the family
orchard to be by himself. Julia, his ten-year-old sister, found him
there. They sat together on a weathered swing, neither of them
able to imagine life without Sam.

Whenever Billy thought of Sam after that, a wave of sadness
washed through him. "My brother was a great favorite with everybody, and his death cast a gloom upon the whole neighborhood,"
Billy said. "It was a terrible blow to all of the family, and especially
to Father, who seemed heartbroken."

But it was Mary Cody who worried everyone, for she could barely
function after her son's death. She was "so affected in health by the
shock of Samuel's death," according to one of Billy's sisters, that
the doctor advised "a change of scene."

Isaac Cody took this advice to heart. Perhaps it would help all of
them, especially his wife, if they moved to a new place where they
had no memories associated with Sam. He started thinking about
Kansas Territory.

Kansas was on the path to statehood. The government was finishing the task of relocating the Indian tribes there to reservations or to other parts of the country, and would soon open the territory to settlement. Those who got there first could stake claims on rich, fertile soil. The eastern part of Kansas Territory had rolling hills, grassy meadows, rivers and streams, and an abundance of birds and game for hunting. The Missouri River formed the border between northeastern Kansas and northwestern Missouri. Isaac wanted to be on the Kansas side of the river, across from the town of Weston, Missouri, where his brother Elijah Cody lived.

Though Isaac knew that Elijah would welcome him in his general store business, Isaac would never consider moving his family to Missouri. It had joined the Union in 1821 as a slave state. In fact, Elijah himself owned slaves. But Isaac did not believe in slavery. He intended to raise his family in a free state, just like Iowa.

And surely Kansans would vote to be free. Missouri's settlers had included Southern planters who had brought their slaves to work on the small plantations they had created in Missouri to produce tobacco and also hemp, which was used to make rope. Kansas had a less temperate climate and wouldn't be suitable for these products. Its appeal was to farmers like Isaac who could handle the rougher terrain and would create farms to grow crops and raise cattle—enterprises less likely to support slavery.

Yes, Isaac decided, Kansas was the place for his family, the promised land where their lives could and would be good again.

Years later, reflecting on what happened to his family, Billy commented, "My father had determined to take up a claim in Kansas and to begin a new life in this stirring country." But, he added, "Had Father foreseen the dreadful consequences to himself and to his family of this decision, we might have remained in Iowa."

CHAPTER 2

ON THE ROAD TO KANSAS

◆ • ◆

Billy's full name was William Frederick Cody. He was born February 16, 1846, in a log cabin near Le Claire, Iowa. Until Sam died, Billy's life had been carefree, much of it spent outdoors, helping on the farm and playing with his brother and sisters.

He was eight in the spring of 1854 when his family set out for Kansas. The month-long journey would take them west across Iowa and then south into Missouri, and finally over the Missouri River into Kansas Territory. Before crossing the river, they planned to stop in Weston, Missouri, to visit Uncle Elijah.

OPPOSITE: Even as a very young child, Billy, shown here at age four, loved animals and the outdoors.

Most settlers headed west in hard, bouncy Conestoga wagons stuffed with their belongings, but Isaac Cody had made enough money selling the Iowa farm that he had a hired man to help with the wagons while Mary and the five girls traveled in the family carriage. Billy rode on horseback, and his dog, Turk, ran along beside him.

With Sam's death, Billy was now the eldest son and was shoul-

Families like the Codys moved slowly and carefully over westward trails.

dering new responsibilities. He knew what his father expected of him. "I was second in command," Billy said, "and I was proud of the job."

Like all frontier boys, Billy had used guns since he'd been old enough to handle them. On the road, both he and his father kept their rifles loaded and ready. They relied on Turk to alert them to danger. Billy felt protective of his mother, his two older sisters—Julia and sixteen-year-old Martha—and his three younger sisters, Eliza, six; Helen, four; and the baby, Mary Hannah.

Some settlers living along the trail opened their homes to travelers, allowing them to spend the night and providing an evening meal and breakfast for a small fee.

When Billy and his family couldn't find a place to stay, they camped out, which pleased Billy very much. He helped unpack the cooking utensils and bedrolls, fed the horses, and searched with his sisters for wood to feed the cooking fire. His favorite time was after everyone was bedded down for the night. As he lay under the stars, his imagination soared. Maybe he would become a plainsman when he grew up. Or a scout on a wagon train, or a mountain man and a

Because their wagons were full of belongings, travelers with no place to stay usually slept under the stars and cooked and ate outside.

trapper. As long as he could live out in the open, hunting for his food and exploring new trails, he would be content.

One time when they stopped to make camp it was still light out, so Billy took Turk hunting, and he shot his first deer. He was already a good fisherman and bird hunter. Even at age eight, he was fearless, which he proved the time Turk got into trouble trying to cross a freezing stream. Billy saw Turk struggling and dove in to rescue him, prompting a witness to say, "I've heard of dogs saving children, but this is the first time I ever heard of a child saving a dog from drowning."

Billy was often likened to his adventure-loving father. As a child, Isaac Cody had emigrated with his family from Canada to Ohio. He was a restless frontiersman, eager to see what was over the next horizon and to turn it into a business venture. In addition to odd jobs, he had worked as a stagecoach driver and had managed farms for other people before becoming a farmer himself.

Billy's mother, Mary, grew up a city girl in Cincinnati, Ohio. Her mother died when she was very young, and her father was killed in a storm at sea when she was fifteen. She loved books and learning, and relatives made certain she received an excellent education. Those who knew her described her as hard working, calm, steadfast, and religious. She was eighteen in 1839 when she took a cruise on a riverboat and met twenty-eight-year-old Isaac. He was on his way to Weston, Missouri, to help his brother Elijah establish his trading post. As Mary soon learned, Isaac had been twice widowed and had a four-year-old daughter, Martha.

They were married the following year and moved to Le Claire, Iowa, to farm. Mary was devoted to Isaac and supported whatever he wanted to do. She loved young Martha as much as the children she and Isaac had together. Her only concern about Billy was that he took little interest in books and education, preferring always to be outdoors. His sister Julia described him as "a genuine child of nature."

Now, heading to Kansas, Billy was in his element. Each day was high adventure. Sometimes he spied deer or buffalo and wished there was time to go hunting. When he and his family came upon other travelers on the trail, he enjoyed talking to them as much as his parents did. He was always on the lookout for good places to stop for the night, imagining that he was a scout and guide, leading the way to Kansas.

"There was something new to be seen at nearly every turn of the road," he said. "The trip proved of interest to all of us, and especially to me."

CHAPTER 3

SLAVERY BECOMES REAL

◆ ◆ ◆

O ne of the things Billy and his sisters missed most on the road to Kansas was bread made of white flour. It was an extravagance for most people, but it was what the Cody children were used to, and they grew tired of the dry cornbread they were offered at most of the farmhouses along the way. Once they stopped at the home of an especially poor family who could offer only two things for dinner: pork fat, and cornbread. Billy tried not to show his disappointment. Happily, when Isaac learned there was a country store nearby, he rode off to purchase food to feed everyone. The store sold freshly baked white bread, just like Mary Cody had always made at home. That night both families had a delicious meal.

After three hundred miles and a month on the road, the Codys were only twenty miles from Weston when Billy spotted "a large and handsome brick residence." He was thinking the same thing as his father, who said, "They probably have white bread there." Billy later recalled the incident in this way: "We drove up to the house and learned that it was owned and occupied by a Mrs. Burns. . . . She was a wealthy lady, and gave us to understand in a pleasant way that she did not entertain travelers. My father, in the course of conversation with her, asked, 'Do you know Elijah Cody?'

"'Indeed I do,' said she. 'He frequently visits us and we visit him. We are the best of friends.'

"'He is a brother of mine,' said father.

"'Is it possible!' she exclaimed. 'Why, you must remain here all night. Have your family come into the house at once. You must not go another step today.'

"This kind invitation was accepted, and we remained there overnight. As father had predicted, we found plenty of white bread at this house, and it proved quite a luxurious treat."

They found something else as well—something they had never encountered before.

"All of the servants were Negro slaves," Julia said. "What impressed [us] was not their different color, but the abject way in which they did the bidding of their mistress, responding quickly—but with heads down—to her every order."

When the family resumed their journey the next day, Billy and his sisters were full of questions. Both Isaac and Mary made it clear that they opposed slavery, but they warned the children that they were going to see slaves at Uncle Elijah's house, too. And would they see slaves in Kansas? Isaac assured them that if they did, they wouldn't for long, since Kansas was going to be a free state.

Privately to Mary, however, Isaac might have expressed his growing concerns. The government had managed to keep the country from going to war over the issue of slavery by maintaining an

Most slaves, including this family owned by a Virginia planter, lived stressful lives filled with hard work and poor food. They could be punished or even sold for any offense.

equal number of slave states and free states. But with Kansas and Nebraska poised to enter the Union, the government was planning to pass the Kansas-Nebraska Act, which would direct settlers to determine by vote if these two states would be free or slave.

Nebraskans were certain to vote free. Nebraska was farther north and did not touch the boundaries of the slave states. Its climate was best suited to ranches and small farms, and the majority of its settlers were immigrants who came from slave-free countries. This meant that the vote in Kansas was crucial to both sides of the slave issue. If Kansas became a slave state, the balance in the US Senate would continue. But if Kansas became a free state, the Senate would have a majority of senators from free states—and one of their first acts could be to ban slavery in the United States.

Although Isaac had been certain that Kansas would be a free state, he had been dismayed to discover that many of the other travelers heading to Kansas were pro-slave, even if they did not own slaves themselves. For the first time he realized that there could be trouble over the issue of slavery. Was he making a mistake by bringing his family here?

———————————

The Codys reached Weston the next day. They easily found Uncle Elijah, for he owned the general store and was a leading merchant, known by everyone in town. Isaac and his brother had not seen each other in over a decade, and, Julia reported, "There was great rejoicing at the reunion."

The family quickly settled in at Elijah's. But the one thing they "could not become accustomed to," said Julia, "was that Uncle Elijah owned slaves, and that we were waited on hand and foot."

That evening the two brothers talked far into the night. They avoided the topic of slavery and instead discussed the other challenges that Kansas presented. The matter of Indians was one of them. Uncle Elijah traded with them, but told Isaac that not all were friendly to whites. They had good reason. Settlers like the Cody's would soon be staking claims on land that had been their home long before the US government began forcing them to relocate to other areas or onto reservations.

Settling close to Fort Leavenworth, which was directly across the river from Weston, would be safest, Uncle Elijah advised.

It was where Isaac had wanted to be all along.

CHAPTER 4

BILLY VISITS FORT LEAVENWORTH

———◆·◆———

Uncle Elijah invited the family to stay with him until Kansas was officially open to settlement. That announcement from the government was expected any day, and in the meantime, Elijah's comfortable home had room for everybody. Billy and his sisters soon knew every nook and corner of the house and grounds. It was time to explore Weston. Billy's sisters asked to go with him, but their mother said no, that it wasn't a proper thing for girls to do, so only Turk went along.

Whenever church bells rang out, Billy knew a steamboat had been spotted approaching the Weston landing, and he and Turk hurried to the docks to watch the unloading of passengers, animals, and cargo. Billy loved all the noise and confusion, the belching smokestacks of the boat, and the shouts of the busy dockworkers

This rare 1854 engraving shows one of the many towns like Weston that were clustered along the banks of the Kansas and Missouri Rivers.

as they rolled barrels full of oysters, peanuts, clothing, and household goods down the gangplank.

The people coming ashore were a mix of businessmen in top hats, ladies dressed in fancy hoop skirts who held parasols to keep the sun off their faces, as well as pioneers clad in work boots and homespun clothing, ready for the next part of their westward migration. When the unloading was done, Billy watched the dockworkers load tobacco, hemp, whiskey, lumber, and hides, all being sent on the return trip to customers back East. All the hustle and bustle was like watching a play unfold—a play with color, action, and excitement.

When Uncle Elijah had arrived in Weston in 1839, it was barely an outpost on the Missouri River. Now, fifteen years later, it was a flourishing town of five thousand and the largest port on the river except for Saint Louis. It was as far west as pioneers from the East could travel by boat. Here in Weston, they purchased wagons, horses, guns and ammunition and other supplies, then crossed the Missouri River by ferry to continue the journey westward on land.

Some set out on their own, while others joined already formed wagon trains that had stopped in Weston to stock up on supplies before they, too, crossed the river and headed out to the unsettled lands beyond. Out there, all pioneers took their chances with rough trails, rattlesnakes, unpredictable weather, and the threat of hostile Indians and outlaws.

Billy envied them. A wagon train! That would be the ultimate

Before bridges were built, travelers hoped to find ferries to get them across rivers. This one operated on the Kansas River.

adventure, and Billy yearned to be the one hitting the trail for parts unknown.

Every time he explored Weston he was impressed by the large homes that some of the well-to-do Southerners had built. They had brought with them their Southern style of architecture, and had adorned their homes with graceful columns, which Billy admired. But they had also brought their slaves, and Billy was at a loss to understand slavery or why his own uncle was a slave owner. He wished he could ask Uncle Elijah, but he knew not to.

The Codys had been in Weston for two weeks when Uncle Elijah announced that he needed to attend to some business matters at Fort Leavenworth in Kansas and invited Isaac and Mary to accompany him. The children were to stay home, but Billy pleaded with his father to be allowed to come. How could there be anything more exciting than seeing an actual military fort? He had to go!

Finally his father gave in, but only for Billy. It would be too much work to bring the girls. They would have to stay behind.

Billy's excitement grew as he and his uncle and parents boarded the ferry with their wagon and horses for the crossing to Kansas. Uncle Elijah told Billy that Fort Leavenworth was located on a prominent point along the Missouri River, close to the Santa Fe and Oregon Trails that were used by pioneers. The fort's presence, and its soldiers constantly going out on patrol, helped protect wagon trains rolling westward.

Fort Leavenworth looked like this when Billy first saw it.

When the fort came into view, Billy gasped. "I shall never forget the thrill that ran through me when Father, pointing at Fort Leavenworth, said, 'Son, you now see a real military fort for the first time in your life.' And a real fort it was!"

Billy could hardly contain his delight when they arrived. "About the post were men dressed all in buckskin with coonskin caps or broad-brimmed slouch hats—real Westerners of whom I had dreamed. Indians of all sorts were about, all friendly, Kickapoo, Pottawatomie, Delaware, Choctaw, and other tribes. Everything I saw fascinated me."

He watched the soldiers with eager attention. "Cavalry were engaged in saber drills, their swords flashing in the sunlight. Artillery was rumbling over the parade ground. Infantry was marching and wheeling." An officer explained that these soldiers might be called upon to fight in Utah, to help subdue the Mormons who were living there and defying the US government by ignoring its laws and instead governing themselves. Or they might be ambushed by outlaws, or attacked by fierce Indian warriors. Danger, it seemed, was everywhere.

"These drills were no fancy dress parades. They meant business," Billy said. "Knowing that the soldiers I saw today might next week be on their way to battle made my eyes big with excitement. I could have stayed there forever."

When Isaac told him it was time to go, Billy reluctantly said his good-byes to everyone he'd met. Leaving the fort, he and his parents and uncle rode through the countryside looking for the perfect place for a farm. Four miles from the fort they climbed a hill and Billy stared in wonder. "From its summit we had a view of the Salt Creek Valley, the most beautiful valley I have ever seen."

Gazing at it, Billy was certain that his father and mother were thinking the same thing he was: this valley would be their new home.

CHAPTER 5

ARRIVING IN THE PROMISED LAND

O nce they descended the steep slope into the Salt Creek Valley, Isaac and Mary quickly found the perfect location for a farm. Billy couldn't imagine a better place anywhere. The valley was nearly twelve miles across and was surrounded by bluffs and rolling hills. Its lush grass was dotted with colorful wildflowers.

Many travelers think of Kansas as flat, but its eastern border has hills and valleys. One of the most beautiful of these areas is the Salt Creek Valley, shown here in an 1867 photo.

It was a busy place. Billy immediately understood why many called it the great gateway to the West, for almost all travelers heading westward entered it after leaving Fort Leavenworth. Billy could see at least a thousand Conestoga wagons. Isaac pointed out some of the traveling groups: Mormons heading to Salt Lake City, fur trappers and pioneers going west, gold prospectors on their way to Oregon or California, and supply trains taking goods to far-flung forts, including Fort Henry in Idaho and Fort Laramie in Wyoming.

"A large number of the wagons, as I learned from my father, belonged to Russell, Majors & Waddell, the great government freighters. They had several trains in the valley, each consisting of twenty-five wagons, heavily loaded with government supplies. . . . Some were being drawn by fifteen yokes of oxen."

Billy rode with his parents and uncle to a nearby store run by a Mr. M. P. Rively. "Perhaps a hundred men, women and children [were] gathered there, engaged in trading and gossiping," Billy said. "The men had huge pistols and knives in their belts; their pants were tucked in their boots, and they wore large broad-rimmed hats. To me they appeared like a lot of cut-throat pirates who had come ashore for a lark. They looked like a very dangerous crowd. Some were . . . drinking whisky freely and becoming intoxicated. It was a busy and an exciting scene."

About a dozen Native Americans were also at the trading post.

Billy was intrigued by their colorful clothing and exotic language. When he realized that they were friendly, he went over and tried to talk to them, but he said the conversation "was very limited."

He could hardly believe his good luck when his parents decided that he could remain in the valley with his father to build a small cabin that would help keep anyone else from trying to stake out the same land before Isaac could file an official claim to it. Since Mary and the girls would be staying in Weston with Uncle Elijah until the cabin was done, Isaac promised that he and Billy would come visit in a few days. That night they had their supper by campfire and slept on the ground. Billy could not have been happier.

The next morning they rode to a Kickapoo village on a nearby Indian reservation. Isaac wanted to meet the government agent living there and inquire about trading with the tribe. When they reached the village, Billy soaked up everything he saw. He admired the Kickapoo homes made of wood and bark, and their big gardens where they grew beans, corn, and squash. He was impressed with the school the children attended. He learned that the tribe was native to Wisconsin but had been forced by the government to relocate several times, this latest time to Kansas Territory. "The Kickapoo were very friendly, and we spent much of our time among them, looking about and studying their habits," Billy said.

Then the best thing happened. Billy's father bought him an Indian pony. It had not been tamed, and Isaac told Billy that it would

Like all Native Americans, the Kickapoo spent most of their time outside their small houses, growing their crops and hunting—primarily buffalo— for food.

be his job to do so. "I made up my mind that I was going to ride that pony or bust," Billy said. He tried over and over again, but the pony kept throwing him off. "I had a couple of hard falls," he said. But he did not intend to give up.

Returning to their camp that afternoon, Billy noticed a group of trappers nearby and walked over to meet them. A young trapper dressed in buckskin was baking bread by wrapping dough around a stick and holding it over burning coals until it was cooked. Billy eagerly accepted the piece the trapper offered him. "Boys are always hungry, but I was especially hungry for such a meal as that," he said. When they finished eating, the trapper walked back with Billy to meet Isaac. "He had a long talk with Father . . . and said that he looked forward with great interest to [going to] Weston, as he expected to meet an uncle, Elijah Cody."

Billy and his father were stunned. "'Elijah Cody!' exclaimed Father. 'Why, Elijah is my brother. I am Isaac Cody. Who are you?'

"'My name is Horace Billings.'

"Isaac's eyes filled with tears. 'You are my nephew. The son of my sister, Sophia.'

"Both men sprang to their feet and began shaking hands in the heartiest manner possible."

Because the family had not heard from Horace in years, Isaac told him that they thought he was dead. Horace shrugged, saying only that since leaving home at a young age, he had been to far-flung places, among them Hawaii and California. "Neither Father nor myself would be satisfied until he had given us a full account of his wanderings and adventures," said Billy, who was fascinated by his tall, handsome cousin.

Horace helped Billy tame his new pony, now named Prince. "With very little trouble Horace rode the peppery little creature this way

Billy tried repeatedly to tame his new pony, but it was his cousin Horace who succeeded.

and that, and at last when he circled back to camp I found that the animal had been mastered," said Billy. "My ambition . . . was to become as skillful a horseman as Horace was."

The following day Billy and Isaac rode to Weston with Horace so he could meet the whole family. Billy's mother suggested that Horace stay for a while and get to know his relatives. Horace agreed. He settled up with the trappers and started to help Isaac and Billy with the cabin.

But Horace found the work tedious. Very quickly he announced that he was going to take a job rounding up horses that had stampeded from Fort Leavenworth the previous spring. The government was paying ten dollars for each horse returned to the fort.

"With father's consent, [Horace] took me with him, and many a wild and perilous chase he led me over the prairie," Billy said. "Whenever Horace caught one of the horses and it would not be led, he immediately threw the horse to the ground and put a saddle and bridle on him. He would then mount the captive horse and ride him into Fort Leavenworth."

Horace's showmanship included grandiose gestures. He didn't just lead a new horse into camp, he'd stand on its back and come racing in at top speed, with a twinkle in his eye and a smart salute to Billy. "Everything that he did, I wanted to do. He was a hero in my eyes, and I wished to follow in his footsteps." Billy said.

"I made rapid advances in the art of horsemanship, for I have had no better teacher than Horace Billings. He taught me how to throw the lasso, which, though difficult to learn, I finally became quite skillful in. . . . At last no more of the horses were to be found. By this time I had become a remarkably good rider."

After Horace was paid for the horses, he returned to help with the cabin. But just as before, the work didn't suit him, and when he struck one of the horses in frustration, Isaac swiftly intervened and gave Horace a sharp lecture about mistreating animals. This rebuke was too much for Horace, and he immediately began packing his things. "That same day," said Billy, "he hired out to a Mormon wagon train, and bidding us all goodbye, started for Salt Lake City." Billy was sorry to see Horace leave, but he understood that building a cabin wasn't a good match for his cousin's restless nature.

When the cabin was almost finished, Isaac started trading goods supplied by Elijah with members of the Kickapoo, Potawatami, Delaware, and Choctaw tribes. The Kickapoo, especially, "became very friendly," Billy said. "Hardly a day passed without a social visit from them. I spent a great deal of time with the Indian boys, who taught me how to shoot with a bow and arrow. I also took part in all their sports, and learned to talk the Kickapoo language."

These sports usually consisted of footraces, competitions to see who could throw stones the longest distance, and games of tag. Billy excelled at all of them.

To celebrate the family's growing friendship with the Kickapoo and some of the other Native Americans, Isaac invited them to a barbecue. Billy's mother, five sisters, Uncle Elijah, and some of his Weston friends came. According to Julia, "The Indians roasted a steer in their own special fashion while the Codys also barbecued an entire beef, using an old family recipe." The Indians were so impressed with how tender and delicious the Cody beef was that they asked how it had been prepared. Mary Cody explained that they had dug a large hole, then covered the meat with hot coals for sixteen hours.

There was other food as well. "Mother made several large boilers full of coffee, which she gave to [the Indians], together with sugar and bread. There were about 200 Indians in attendance at the feast, and they all enjoyed and appreciated it," Billy said.

Indians were rarely invited to such events, and they showed their gratitude by performing a ceremonial war dance around the evening fire. Billy's sister Julia understood the significance. "In the lands to the north and west, these very rites were being danced in dead seriousness, out of hatred for the white man," she said.

"At the barbecue, however, war paint and battle headdress were mere theatrical trappings, meant to thrill and not to frighten the onlookers."

And Billy was thrilled by it, for he was witnessing something he would love all his life: drama and pageantry. Like Horace Billings, the Indians were skilled showmen, and just as he had been with his daring cousin, eight-year-old Billy Cody was their eager student.

CHAPTER 6

AT HOME IN THE VALLEY

◆·◆

That spring of 1854 was momentous both for the Codys and for the future state of Kansas. On May 30, just a month after the family had first arrived at Uncle Elijah's home in Weston, Congress passed the Kansas-Nebraska Act, opening both territories to settlement—the first step to statehood. As soon as they heard, the Codys rushed to the land office at Fort Leavenworth. With his mother and sisters, Billy watched with excitement as Isaac filled out the paperwork to officially claim their section of prime Salt Creek Valley land, relieved that no one contested them for it. The land was theirs!

According to Julia, "the Codys had the honor of being the first to file . . . in the entire Kansas Territory. This first land patent [was] signed by President Franklin Pierce himself."

Isaac was full of optimism. The family was slowly recovering from Sam's death nine months earlier, and Mary Cody was expecting a baby. Now, with their 160 acres in the beautiful Salt Creek Valley, everything seemed possible. The family moved into the newly completed cabin and Isaac started to work on a two-story, seven-room wood-frame house that would be one of the nicest in the whole area. He secured a contract with Fort Leavenworth to supply two thousand tons of hay each year, at fifteen dollars per ton, to help feed the fort's many animals. That still left enough land to plant a field of corn and to also create a huge garden.

Though the Codys were among the very first settlers in the valley, new neighbors began moving onto claims and starting their own farms. Isaac had been trained as a surveyor, and some of these neighbors hired him to establish property lines so they would not face disputes about who had rights to their land. This was necessary because squatters were also moving in and staking illegal claims so they could vote. Most squatters were from western Missouri and wanted Kansas to be a slave state. No one asked if they intended to build a house and actually live on the land, and they hoped that when it was time to vote, no one would ask if they lived in Kansas or Missouri.

"Some of these Missourians staked out a piece of property with whiskey bottles, daring anyone to take it from them," Julia said. "They carried guns in their belts and bowie knives in their boots."

To protect their illegal claims, squatters banded together in pro-slave organizations that could quickly turn violent.

It wasn't just the squatters who were pro-slave. As Isaac now knew, so were many of his neighbors who had filed legal claims and planned to stay. Isaac kept his politics to himself, but he was realizing more and more that it was going to take a big fight to make Kansas a free state.

With so many people pouring into Kansas Territory, towns sprang up. The first was Leavenworth, several miles from Fort Leavenworth. Within five years it would not only be the headquarters for the massive overland shipping company of Russell, Majors & Waddell, but it would also have five thousand citizens, making it the largest town in Kansas. Another new town was Lawrence, forty-five miles to the southwest of Leavenworth on the Kansas River. Its first residents were abolitionists from the East who were ready to take a stand against slavery in Kansas.

The abolitionists coming into the territory were of special concern to pro-slavers since they helped slaves escape from their masters. The Underground Railroad was already active in Iowa, which was north of Missouri, and in Illinois, which was Missouri's neighbor to the east. The majority of Missouri's slaves were the property of farmers and planters who lived along the western border that Missouri shared with Kansas. If Kansas became a free state, Missouri slaves had only to cross the border to reach freedom.

Isaac was committed to Kansas being free, but he had far too much work to do to get involved in the conflict. "He minded his own business," said Billy, "and avoided all the factional disputes with which the neighborhood abounded." Along with his work as a surveyor and farmer, Isaac started a store with Uncle Elijah, stocking it with goods and merchandise from Elijah's business in Weston. Even though Rively's store was only two miles away and was much better established, Isaac and Elijah's store soon gave it stiff competition.

By 1858, Leavenworth was the largest town between Saint Louis and San Francisco. Many of its original buildings are still standing.

Their customers were mostly their neighbors and also the Kickapoo. "On Saturday night the squaws visited the Cody store," Julia said, "their ponies laden down with packs of fresh garden vegetables to trade for beads, calico, jewelry and trinkets. During the week the braves came . . . bringing furs, hides, horses and handicraft work. They left with saddles, household articles, medicine, chewing tobacco, candy and many other items, either useful or decorative, which caught their fancy."

Everyone in the family shared the work, and there was plenty of it. Billy and his older sisters helped with all the chores and worked in the fields and the garden. They also helped out at the store. Billy drove the supply wagon back and forth to Uncle Elijah's store in Weston to get supplies—a big job for an eight-year-old, since it meant crossing on the ferry with the wagon and horses, loading all the goods into the wagon, and then recrossing the river, driving the wagon to the

store, and unloading everything. But Billy liked the challenge and was proud that he could already do the work of a man.

Mary Cody wanted her children to be educated and talked about getting a school started as soon as possible, but it was Billy's opinion that he was already getting all the education he needed for the life he wanted. Because the Cody farm was prominently situated in the valley, travelers often stopped for water and a short rest. Whenever Billy's responsibilities allowed, he took time to visit with them. He asked where they were headed and how long it would take them to get there. He was especially interested in folks returning from the West—which was any place west of the Salt Creek Valley. Were there any towns yet? Had they seen

Thousands of travelers passed through the Salt Creek Valley, heading west along the trails or looking for land in Kansas Territory.

buffalo? Had they visited a fort? Had they encountered Indians, and were they hostile or friendly? What were the mountains like? He longed to see that far country with his own eyes and to explore its many wonders.

He loved riding his pony, Prince, around the valley, which gave him the opportunity to stop and talk to people, and he happily did errands for his father that allowed him to get out and about. He was always on the lookout for William Russell, a partner in the overland freight company headquartered in Leavenworth, so he could hear him talk about his overland freighting company's huge wagon trains rolling westward. Russell regaled Billy with stories of outlaws and surprise Indian attacks, of crossing the mountains in sudden blizzards, of landslides and fording dangerous rivers. Billy soaked it all up. "[Mr. Russell] seemed to take a considerable interest in me," he said. "I became acquainted with many wagon masters, hunters and teamsters, and learned a great deal about the business of handling cattle and mules."

Billy would always miss his big brother, Sam, but he was glad they had left Iowa, for he wanted to be a plainsman or a scout and to someday live out on the farthest western frontier. He cherished the life his family was creating in Kansas. He had his dog, Turk, and his pony, Prince. His father was prosperous, and the family's new home was large and comfortable and filled with love, laughter, and good times. And, best of all, their new baby would soon be born.

Neither Billy nor any of his family could know that ill winds were blowing and that a firestorm of conflict was about to ignite in their valley, changing their lives forever.

CHAPTER 7

ISAAC CODY'S BLOODY TRAIL

◆◆◆

The Codys had been in the Salt Creek Valley barely three months when, one day in September 1854, eight-year-old Billy and his father passed Rively's store on the way home from a trip to Fort Leavenworth.

The owner, M. P. Rively, had declared himself to be pro-slave, and his store had become the headquarters for pro-slave men. Because Isaac's brother Elijah was a slaveholder, "for a time it was taken for granted that Father held the same views," Billy said. Word gradually got out, however, and although Isaac tried to get along with everyone, he did not deny his anti-slave beliefs. Billy said of his father, "He was never at any pains to hide his own opinions, being a man who was afraid of nothing."

At Rively's that day, said Billy, "We saw a crowd of drunken horsemen . . . yelling and shooting their pistols in the air. They caught sight of us immediately, and a few of them advanced toward us. Father expected trouble, but he was not a man to turn back."

The men, who were on foot, ignored Billy and surrounded Isaac, accusing him of being an abolitionist and demanding that he declare his views. "By this time more than a dozen men had crowded about Father, cursing and abusing him. Soon they tore him from his horse. One of them rolled a dry goods box from the store." Billy watched helplessly as they forced his father to stand on it. They passed around liquor bottles and hurled insults at Isaac.

Billy saw his father survey the mob "with no fear." He held his breath as his father began to speak. "I am not ashamed of my views," Isaac declared. "I am not an abolitionist, and never have been. I think it is better to let slavery alone in the states where it is now. But I am not afraid to tell you that I am opposed to its extension, and that I believe it should be kept out of Kansas."

This made the men angrier. Isaac's speech was followed by "a wild yell of derision. Men began crowding around him, cursing and shaking their fists." Suddenly, Billy said, a man named Charles Dunn "jumped up on the box. . . . I saw the gleam of a knife. The next instant, without a groan, Father fell forward." With a cry of shock, Billy rushed to catch his father, almost collapsing under his weight. Isaac was bleeding badly, and as Billy carefully eased him to the ground, he saw Dunn approaching with his knife.

Billy could do nothing to help when his father was stabbed.

Someone yelled, "Look out, [you'll] stab the kid!" Before Billy could react, one of the men restrained Dunn, pulling him away.

Rively broke up the crowd and helped Billy get his father into the safety of the store. While a messenger hurried to the Cody farm to tell Mary what had happened, Billy tried to stop the bleeding. He was terrified that his father would die. Each moment waiting for his mother felt like an eternity, but finally she came rushing in. Ignoring the taunts of the drunken men standing around, Rively and several others helped get Isaac into the Cody wagon.

Billy crawled into the back with Isaac and cradled his head while Mary pushed the horses as hard as she could over the rough roads to the ferry for the crossing to Weston, where there was a doctor. But could they get there in time? Billy was certain his father would die. "I believed he was mortally wounded," he said. Sam had died just a year ago. Would they lose Father, too?

At Elijah's home, the doctor tended to Isaac. Days passed, and then weeks. "Mother nursed Father carefully," Billy said, until finally the doctor told them Isaac would live. But one lung had been punctured in the attack and the doctor was unable to say whether Isaac would ever fully recover.

With conflict increasing between pro- and anti-slave factions, no one dared pursue Charles Dunn. A week after the stabbing, a pro-slave newspaper editor in nearby Liberty, Missouri, reported the incident this way:

A Mr. Cody, a noisy abolitionist, living near Salt Creek, in Kansas Territory, was severely stabbed, while in dispute about a claim with Mr. Dunn, on Monday last week. Cody is severely hurt, but not enough it is feared to cause his death. The settlers of Salt Creek regret that his wound is not more dangerous, and all sustain Mr. Dunn in the course he took.

It didn't matter that the truth was that some of Isaac's Salt Creek neighbors supported him, or that Isaac was a "free state" man and not an abolitionist: if you did not support slavery, you were considered an abolitionist, and that was that.

According to Julia, Isaac Cody was the first man in Kansas to shed blood for the free-state cause. "The path over which he was borne by wagon after the assault at Rively's is called 'Cody Bloody Trail' in early histories of Kansas," she said. "The attack on him marked the opening of undeclared war in the territory—a war in which wanton destruction was to be thrust upon the weak and the defenseless."

Back home to begin a long period of recovery, Isaac received continual threats from pro-slavers demanding that he leave the territory. "He was threatened with death by hanging or shooting if he dared to remain," said Billy. But Isaac refused to be terrorized. He had a farm and several businesses to manage. He had six children to care for and a baby on the way. He had worked hard to create a new life for his family in the Salt Creek Valley. Surely the animosity would die down.

But several nights later, as eight-year-old Billy and twelve-year-old Julia were returning to the house on horseback, Julia said they "saw some men racing along the stacks of piled-up hay, applying torches to the dried grass." They rushed home to sound the alarm, but it was too late. With their stunned parents, they stood on the front stoop and wept as they watched the fields burn.

"Months of effort went up in smoke," said Julia. "Several hundred tons [of hay]—representing in part the money the family desperately needed to pay Father's considerable medical expenses—were reduced to a handful of dust."

A few nights after the hay burning, Billy spied a gang of men on horseback approaching the house. He hurried to warn his mother. On the violent American frontier, men usually spared women and children. Hoping that this would hold true, Mary hastily helped Isaac put on a long skirt and big broad-brimmed sunbonnet. She was wrapping a large shawl around him just as the men arrived.

Mary and the children could not risk trying to help Isaac as he struggled to stay on his feet. "Carrying a water pail in one hand and gripping a revolver under his shirt with the other, he walked slowly out into the yard and entered a nearby cornfield, unchallenged by the riders," Julia said. As the men dismounted and questioned Mary about her husband's whereabouts, Isaac stayed hidden in the tall, thick corn.

"Mother very truthfully told them that he was away," said Billy. "They were not satisfied with her statement, however, and they at once made a thorough search of the house. They raved and swore when they could not find him, and threatened him with death whenever they should catch him."

The men ordered Mary to fix food for them while they waited for Isaac to

While women sometimes disguised themselves as men so they could fight, men sometimes disguised themselves as women to avoid violence and capture.

return. The night had grown chilly and damp, and while Mary tried to humor the men, Billy sneaked out of the house with several blankets, taking Turk with him. In the pitch-black night the dog led the way through the cornfield until, finally, they found Isaac. Billy gave his shivering father the blankets and then hurriedly rejoined his mother before the men noticed his absence. At last they grew tired of waiting and left, threatening that they'd be back.

"I am sure if they had captured Father that night they would have killed him," Billy said. "They carried off nearly everything of value and drove off all the horses." When Billy learned that his own pony had been taken, he was heartbroken.

But at least for the moment, Isaac was safe. The family helped him back into the house for the night, though at dawn he had to return to the cornfield for safety. Billy kept a careful eye on the road. "My first real work as a scout began [during this time] for I had to keep constantly on the watch for raids by ruffians, who had sworn that Father must die."

The next day, Mary Cody sent Billy to Rively's store on the pretext of buying groceries, but in reality to see what he could learn. Billy overheard several men talking of their plans to find and kill Isaac. So in spite of his weak condition, Isaac was forced to stay in the cornfield. His family made him a bed of hay and blankets and brought him food. But his health deteriorated and he suffered from chills and fever. He needed medical attention.

He and Mary decided that he must try to get to Fort Leavenworth. He would be safe there and could get medical care.

Once Isaac was ready to depart, he called the family to him. He placed his hand gently on Billy's head and said he was counting on his boy to take care of his mother and sisters.

Because all their horses had been stolen, Isaac would have to walk the four miles to the fort. He bid the family farewell, and as he set out on foot under the cover of darkness, they watched from the porch until they could no longer see him. Billy's sister Helen never forgot the sadness they all felt: "None of us knew whether we should ever again see our father."

CHAPTER 8

PRO-SLAVE OR FREE STATE?

◆·•·◆

Afew days later the family received word through friends that Isaac had reached Fort Leavenworth safely. Now they had to carry on while he was gone—and nothing was going well. The farm was all but ruined. They still had their store, but their customers were mostly their Native American friends, for their pro-slave neighbors now shopped exclusively at Rively's.

Worst of all, the valley had exploded in violence. At any time of day or night, raiders crossed the border from Missouri, bent on terrorizing free-state settlers. In response, free-staters formed vigilante bands to protect their property and to strike out at pro-slave settlers. One pro-slaver wrote his family back East that "I have my rifle, revolver, and pistol where I can lay my hand on them in an instant, besides a hatchet & axe. I take this precaution to guard against the midnight attacks of the Abolitionists, who never make an attack in open daylight and no pro-slavery man knows when he is safe here in the Territory."

Whichever side you were on, you were at risk. Billy heard about an abolitionist lawyer in Leavenworth who was tarred, feathered, and run out of town. In pro-slave Atchison, Kansas, a newly established village just eighteen miles from Weston, Missouri, a minister had dared to speak out against slavery. Pro-slavers tied him to a raft in the Missouri River and a mob threw stones at him. The Atchison newspaper editorialized that "this same punishment we will award to all free-soilers, abolitionists, and their emissaries."

President Pierce hoped that setting up a territorial government would quell the violence, and he appointed a Pennsylvania lawyer named Andrew Horatio Reeder to be the first territorial governor. Reeder held an election for Kansas voters that fall of 1854 to choose their first congressman.

Determined that Kansas would become a slave state, Missourians crossed the state line to vote illegally in territorial elections.

But pro-slave Missourians poured over the border to stuff Kansas ballot boxes, saying they lived in Kansas. Billy and his family were hardly surprised when the pro-slave candidate won by a landslide.

Shortly after the election, Billy and his mother and sisters welcomed Isaac home from his two-month stay at Fort Leavenworth. He still suffered from occasional infection and fever, but from now on, no matter what happened or what threats he received, he told his family that he was going to work for the free-state cause. Pro-slavers would not win, he resolved. Kansas would be free!

Brushing off the family's worries about his health and safety, Isaac traveled to Lawrence, the free-state capital of the territory, to get acquainted with abolitionist leaders and assure them of his support. Pro-slavers heard about this and shook their heads. Hadn't that thickheaded abolitionist learned his lesson? This time the family's livestock were driven off or killed. Then, one evening when Isaac was in bed, ill with fever, an old judge rode up to the house. He had been at Rively's store and had cheered loudly when Isaac was stabbed. Billy just stared: the judge was riding his pony, Prince!

The judge drank liberally from a flask of whiskey as he pushed his way into the house. Threatening pregnant Mary with a bowie knife, he ordered her to cook a meal for him. Mary set to work, trying to conceal her fear that Isaac would be discovered upstairs. The judge sat at the kitchen table. He waved his knife at the children and told them he was going to search the house and would kill their father if he found him.

Eight-year-old Billy wasn't going to let that happen. "Now, I knew something about a gun, and there was a gun handy, and I lost no time in getting it. Sitting on the stairs, I cocked it and held it across my knees."

The judge kept an eye on Billy, taunting him with his knife. "I'm going to finish up the job that Charlie Dunn began," he slurred. Mary set a full plate of food before him. Forgetting everything else, he plowed into his meal, washing it down with more whiskey. Then he rose unsteadily, lurched outside, climbed onto Prince, and started to ride off.

Billy sprang into action. He whistled for Turk and ordered the dog to attack. Turk chased the old man, snarling and lunging at his leg. The judge tried to beat him off, but Turk wouldn't let up. Finally the judge slid off Prince, his pant leg shredded and bloodied. Too drunk to protest what was happening, he staggered on down the road, while Prince trotted back to an elated Billy.

After this incident, the Codys had to face reality. "Father could be of no service to us," Billy said. "His presence, in fact, was a menace." Isaac needed a way to make some income and a safe place to stay while he continued to recover. When he was contacted by free-state men asking him to locate land and lay out a new free-state community, he and Mary decided that this was the solution.

Late that fall of 1854, thirty miles from the Salt Creek Valley, Isaac chose a spot for the new town and named it Grasshopper Falls, the same name the Native Americans had given a nearby waterfall. Realizing that the falls could power a sawmill for lumber and a gristmill to grind grain, he hired workers and began supervising construction.

Back at the farm, the family kept Isaac's whereabouts a secret and struggled along without him. All winter they relied on Uncle Elijah to send them provisions from Weston since Isaac was not yet making any money. Billy took Turk hunting every day to supply rabbits and birds for food. He and his sisters ground corn to make flour. Less than a year earlier they had complained about having to eat dry, tasteless cornbread during their journey from Iowa to Kansas. Now they were thankful to have it.

Pro-slave men regularly showed up looking for Isaac. They took what they wanted and often demanded to be fed. Mary did her best. All around them, families were moving away, unable to deal with the violence any longer. In fact, at least half of the early settlers left the territory because of it.

Even with a baby coming, Mary refused to flee. Elijah tried to persuade her to bring the children and live in Weston, but, Billy said, "Mother had made up her mind not to be driven out. . . . She said that the pro-slavery men had taken everything except the land and [our] home, and she proposed to remain there as long as she lived, happen what might." Elijah was also threatened by pro-slavers for helping his brother's family. He "could not assist us much," said Billy, "beyond expressing his sympathy and sending us provisions."

When Isaac came home, he arrived under the cover of darkness and left a day or two later before sunrise. But with winter making travel difficult, his visits were few. During his absences Billy and his sisters relied heavily on their mother. Julia said their mother was a "quiet presence" they could turn to for help in solving problems and that each evening she read to them from the Bible. "Kindness, consideration, love, and the word of the Good

Like the children in this painting, Billy and his sisters were more dependent than ever on their mother whenever their father was away.

Book—these were the things on which she based her life, these were the legacies she [passed on to us]."

Billy turned nine in February 1855, and a month later voters went back to the polls to elect representatives to the new territorial legislature. According to Julia, "Again an army of Missourians invaded Kansas and marched in force to the polling places at Lawrence. Armed with pistols, rifles and knives—and even dragging two cannons loaded with musket-balls through the streets—they stormed the [voting] booths." Once more, pro-slavery candidates won by a landslide. The new legislature, Julia said, "soon made it a criminal act for anyone to speak against slavery or to advocate free-soil policies in Kansas."

In response, Eastern abolitionists stepped up their support. Henry Ward Beecher was one of them. He was a minister and the brother of Harriet Beecher Stowe, the author of *Uncle Tom's Cabin*. Comparing the free-state cause in Kansas to a holy war, the Reverend Beecher raised funds to send abolitionists in Lawrence several hundred Sharps rifles—considered the best rifles to be had.

The rifles became known as "Beecher's Bibles," for they were shipped under the noses of Missourians in boxes marked "Books." When they arrived, Kansas abolitionists were ready to fight.

OPPOSITE: The Reverend Beecher received death threats from Southerners whenever he spoke out against slavery or helped raise money to purchase freedom for slaves.

CHAPTER 9

BILLY SOUNDS THE ALARM

◆·◆

In the midst of all the troubles, the Codys had cause to rejoice. In May 1855, Mary gave birth to Charles Whitney Cody—Charlie, for short. Isaac came home to meet his new son and to celebrate with the family. But the threats against his life quickly resumed, and he had to return to the safety of Grasshopper Falls.

Mary and the children kept on. Working the fields was one of their hardest tasks, especially now that pro-slavers had destroyed or stolen most of their farm equipment. They still had a small plow. Nine-year-old Billy was determined to get some crops growing, so he hooked up Prince and together they managed to plant some corn. Kansas's skies were dry that summer and there wouldn't be much of a crop, but Billy knew they desperately needed anything that grew. They had only two cows left, and he drove them to pasture each day. He took along his gun for target practice. Sometimes two Kickapoo boys he'd become friends with would join him from their nearby reservation, and their company helped him pass the time.

He saw the worry in his mother's eyes. In addition to her concerns for her family's safety, she had baby Charlie to care for. She also had to rely on Uncle Elijah to send provisions from Weston to help feed the family. Billy wondered if he could hire out to help other farmers—not that they'd be able to pay much of anything.

One day his old friend William Russell stopped to visit. Billy poured out the family's troubles. "'Billy, my boy,' said Russell, 'cheer up and come to Leavenworth and I'll employ you. I'll give you twenty-five dollars a month to herd cattle.'"

Billy considered what such a sum would mean to his mother. Full of excitement, "I accepted the offer, and, heartily thanking him, hurried home to obtain mother's consent." But Mary Cody wasn't about to allow her nine-year-old son to leave home to work, not even to earn badly needed income. Billy argued that his sisters could do the farm chores and that Russell had assured him he would be in no danger. To Billy's dismay, "She refused to let me go, and all my pleading was in vain."

He thought hard about it. Then, he said, he "stole away and walked to Leavenworth," trusting that his mother would understand.

When he reported to the freight company's headquarters, Russell followed through on his promise. He gave Billy a horse and sent him out to the countryside to look after the company's cattle. Billy later learned that as soon as he left, Russell went to see Mary Cody to tell her where Billy was and to assure her that he'd look after the boy. Mary Cody finally gave in, touched by her son's determination to help.

The rest of the summer Billy worked alongside several other herders as they moved the cattle from one grazing site to another to fatten them for market. At night the herders ate by firelight and slept under the stars. Billy missed his family and worried about his father's health and safety. But otherwise, it was the perfect life.

At the end of the season the herders drove the cattle into Leavenworth, and Billy received his wages for two months: fifty dollars, paid out in half-dollar pieces. It was the most money he had ever seen at one time. "I put the bright silver coins into a sack . . . and started home, thinking myself a millionaire. This money I gave to Mother, who had already forgiven me for running away."

When Isaac arrived home for a brief visit, talk got around to the political news in the territory, none of it good. The pro-slave legislature had moved its meeting site close to the Missouri border to make it more convenient for Missourians to attend. The site was the Shawnee Indian Mission, run by Thomas Johnson, a Methodist missionary from Virginia who had brought his slaves with him when he settled in Kansas. It was located on the Santa Fe Trail and was very close to the pro-slave town of Westport, Missouri, just across the border from Kansas.

Meeting at the Mission, the pro-slave legislature passed laws making it illegal to write or speak against slavery. They called for the death penalty for anyone convicted of freeing slaves. And they declared slavery to be official in Kansas.

Isaac was disgusted with this turn of events. In response, he

***

OPPOSITE: This painting shows an older herder doing the same work that Billy did at age nine. Herders endured heat, wind, rain, stampedes, and the threat of rattlesnakes.

THE DAY OF
OUR ENSLAVEMENT!!

To-day, Sept. 15, 1855, is the day on which the ini-

quitous enactment of an illegitimate, illegal and fraudulent Legislature have declared commences the prostration of the **Right of Speech** and the curtailment of the **LIBERTY OF THE PRESS**!! To-day commences an Era in **Kansas** which, unless the sturdy voice of the People, backed, if necessary, by "strong arms and the sure eye," shall teach the tyrants who attempt to enthrall us the lesson which our Fathers taught to kingly tyrants of old, shall prostrate us in the dust, and make us the slaves of an Oligarchy

Worse than the veriest Despotism on Earth!

To-day commences the operation of a law which declares: "**Sec. 12.** If any free person, by speaking or by writing, assert or maintain that persons have not the right to hold slaves in this Territory, or shall introduce into this Territory, print, publish, write, circulate or cause to be introduced into this Territory, written, printed, published or circulated in this Territory, any book, paper, magazine, pamphlet or circular, containing any denial of the right of persons to hold slaves in this Territory, such person shall be deemed guilty of Felony, and punished by imprisonment at hard labor for a term of not less than two years."

Now we DO ASSERT and we declare, despite all the

bolts and bars of the iniquitous Legislature of Kansas, that

"PERSONS HAVE NOT THE
RIGHT TO HOLD SLAVES IN THIS
TERRITORY."

And we will emblazon it upon our banner in letters so large and in language so plain that the infatuated invaders who elected the Kansas Legislature, as well as

THAT CORRUPT AND IGNORANT LEGISLATURE

Itself, may understand it--- so that, if they cannot read,

they may **SPELL IT OUT**, and meditate and deliberate upon it; and we hold that the man who fails to utter this self-evident truth, on account of the insolent enactment alluded to, is a poltroon and a slave worse than the black slaves of our persecutors and oppressors.

The Constitution of the United States, the great Magna Charta of American Liberties,

Guarantees to every Citizen the Liberty of Speech and
the Freedom of the Press!

And this is the first time in the history of America that a body claiming Legislative powers has dared to attempt to wrest them from the people. And it is not only the right, but the bounden duty of every Freeman to spurn with contempt and trample under foot an enactment which thus basely violates the rights of Freemen. For our part we **DO** and **SHALL CONTINUE** to utter this truth so long as we have the power of utterance, and nothing but the brute force of an overbearing tyranny can prevent us.

Will any citizen --- any free American --- brook the insult of

AN INSOLENT GAG LAW!!

the work of a Legislature elected by bullying ruffians who invaded Kansas with arms, and whose drunken revelry, and insults to our peaceable, unoffending, and comparatively unarmed citizens, were a disgrace to manhood, and a burlesque upon popular Republican Government! If they do, they are slaves already, and with them Freedom is but a mockery.

and others who shared his views organized the Free State Party to oppose the pro-slavers. They determined they would select their own representative to Congress and send this person immediately to Washington, DC.

That fall of 1855 the Free State Party met in Topeka, a growing anti-slave community west of Lawrence. Isaac helped draft a constitution for his party that openly defied the pro-slave constitution. In the next election a majority of Kansans voted to adopt the Free State Party's Topeka Constitution, creating a second government in Kansas. Julia said that Kansas Territory now had "two legislatures, each refusing to accept the authority of the other, and each claiming to represent the 'real' sentiment of the people." Somehow this mess had to be straightened out if Kansas was ever going to be able to join the Union.

OPPOSITE: This poster was published in Lawrence, Kansas, in 1855, in response to the news that the pro-slave legislature had declared slavery to be official in Kansas. ABOVE: In addition to white males, the Topeka Constitution granted voting rights to "civilized" male Indians, meaning those who lived and acted like white men.

Isaac was becoming well known as a champion of the free-state cause. New free-state settlers arriving in the area wanted to meet him and often stopped for a few days at the Codys' farm. Whether Isaac was there or not, Mary Cody welcomed them, sharing what meager food the family had and inviting them to sleep in the house. When there was no more room, the settlers slept in the yard, either in tents or their wagons.

Pro-slavers were now more committed than ever to silencing Isaac. One day two of them sneaked into the mill at Grasshopper Falls and struck Isaac on the head, knocking him unconscious. Luckily, he wasn't seriously injured. But this incident was yet another worry for Billy. Whenever his father was home, he kept careful watch over him. "Not a day or night went by that Billy, in his role of 'scout,' did not see horsemen silhouetted against the sky watching the Cody farm," Julia said.

Even with all this going on, Mary Cody pressured Isaac to find a teacher so they could at last start a school. Billy didn't like the idea of sitting still to study, but he knew that his mother couldn't be talked out of it.

Isaac gave in. Through contacts he located a young teacher back East, Miss Jennie Lyons, who was willing to come start a school. Several free-state neighbor children and Billy's two Kickapoo pals, who rode on horseback early mornings from the reservation, joined the Cody children for daily classes in the old cabin on the Codys' property.

Billy liked his teacher, and to everyone's surprise, he worked hard for her. For several months "the little school at home got along exceedingly well," Billy said, "and we all made rapid advances in our studies as Miss Lyons was an excellent teacher."

But pro-slavers objected to the school. According to Julia, "Miss Lyons carried on the work of the school under great hardships. Again and again pro-slavers on horseback paid visits to her classroom and informed her of how they felt about Isaac Cody and that they didn't intend to allow 'that old abolition cuss to teach sedition to our youngsters.'"

Finally the pressure became too much for the young woman and she returned to the East. Billy was sorry to see her go, but he was glad to once again spend his days outside doing chores.

One morning he was sick in bed with the flu. Suddenly a family friend rushed into the house, warning that a gang of pro-slavers had just left the valley, headed to Grasshopper Falls to kill Isaac.

Billy threw on his clothes, determined to warn his father. His mother tried to stop him. It was a thirty-mile ride, she said, and Billy was far too ill to make it. But nine-year-old Billy refused to listen and was soon on his way. Though he was feverish, light-headed, and so sick to his stomach that he vomited on Prince, he was also determined.

When he reached the halfway point at Stranger Creek, he saw some men ahead of him who had stopped to water their horses. He figured they must be the gang. Giving them wide berth, Billy stayed behind the trees and inched Prince forward as quietly as possible until he would be able to pass them. Then one of the men shouted, "That's Cody's boy!"

They ordered Billy to halt. "A pistol shot, to terrify me into obedience, accompanied the command. I may have been terrified, but it was not into obedience," Billy said. "I instantly started my pony on a run, and on looking back I saw that I was being pursued by three or four of the party . . . no doubt supposing that they could easily capture me."

Several times Billy heard shots. He pressed on. "I urged Prince to his utmost speed, feeling that upon him and myself depended a life that was dearer to me than that of any other man in the world."

Billy held on tight. "I led my pursuers on a lively chase for four or five miles; finally, when they saw they could not catch me, they [stopped]." Billy pressed ahead. "I kept straight on to Grasshopper Falls," he said, "arriving there in ample time to inform father of the approach of his old enemies."

Isaac quickly alerted the men in the mill to be on guard. Then he put his sick son to bed, proud of what Billy had done that day.

OPPOSITE: Billy was used to riding long distances—he often traveled thirty miles a day doing errands—but never when he was so ill, much less when being chased by pro-slavers.

CHAPTER 10

BILLY MEETS THE ABOLITIONISTS

◆·◆

The pro-slave gang returned to the Salt Creek Valley and let it be known that they would eventually get Isaac—and that they were now keeping an eye on Billy. Was the code of not harming women and children changing? The Kansas-Missouri border had become so violent that no one really knew what the "rules" were anymore, especially when they involved a boy like Billy.

Isaac felt that as soon as Billy recovered from the flu they should go to Lawrence for a few days until this latest incident died down. They would both be safe there, and Isaac could finish up some political work.

While his father attended to business, Billy explored Lawrence. He liked that its first thirty-two streets were named for states already in the Union. He admired the Victorian-style brick homes of well-to-do residents. He strolled down Massachusetts Street, named for the home state of the New England Emigrant Aid Company—the abolitionist organization responsible for the creation of Lawrence. Businesses lining the street included the Free State Hotel, the tallest building in town. Lawrence had two newspapers and a school, and it was home to Plymouth Congregational Church—one of the first organized churches in Kansas. One proud citizen said, "Lawrence is the commercial, literary, and political center of the State. More building going on here than in any other place west of the Mississippi!"

At one end of town, Billy watched the boat traffic along the Kansas River. At the other end, he climbed Mount Oread, the prominent

In this woodcut of early Lawrence, the Free State Hotel is the building with the flag on top.

hill named for the home of one of the emigrant company's founders. Climbing to the summit, he could see for miles. Lookouts kept watch there for approaching border ruffians. It's likely they told Billy about the parade that had been held on the Fourth of July, when residents sang patriotic songs and proudly showed off the

powerful new Sharps rifles sent by Henry Ward Beecher. Billy toured the earthwork fortifications and watched men practicing militia drills. Most people thought it was just a matter of time before pro-slavers mounted an attack on the town.

Three of the Lawrence abolitionist leaders especially impressed Billy. Charles Robinson was a Massachusetts native and a medical doctor who had been sent a year earlier by the emigrant company to start the town. Robinson had named it for Amos Lawrence, a founder of the emigrant company. Robinson was in his late thirties and had a quiet manner and dignified

The abolitionist Charles Robinson founded Lawrence, Kansas. He and his wife, Sara, were both active in the free-state cause. Robinson became the first governor of the state of Kansas.

air. He always looked for peaceful resolutions to conflict, though he was willing to fight when necessary.

Billy also met Jim Lane, an Indiana lawyer in his early forties who had recently arrived in Lawrence to work for the abolitionist cause. He was tall and gaunt, with prominent cheekbones and wild hair that stuck out in every direction. He dressed in outlandish outfits, including a bearskin overcoat that he wore even in the summer. He was friendly, but he had a terrible temper. He was known as a powerful speaker who could sway audiences, waving his long arms and shrieking "Great God!" for emphasis.

Lane and Robinson clashed in both personality and approach. Each wanted to be the leader of the newly formed Free State Party. Unlike Robinson, Lane promoted the use of force in the fight to make Kansas free.

Jim Lane used violence in his quest to make Kansas a free state. His behavior could be so outlandish that many people thought he was mentally unstable.

The third leader was John Brown. He lived near Osawatomie, fifty miles away, but he was often in Lawrence because of his alliance with Jim Lane. If ever there was a radical abolitionist, it was John Brown. Born in 1800 in Connecticut, Brown and his seven brothers and sisters grew up in a deeply religious Protestant family. Brown often quoted the Bible to justify his actions.

When he was twelve he was friends with a slave boy the same age. One day he watched helplessly as the boy was beaten bloody by his master for some supposed infraction. From then on, Brown dedicated his life to ending slavery. He felt this could only happen through violence. When he arrived in Kansas the spring of 1855, he brought along a wagonload of guns, knives, and sabers.

Brown had remarried after the death of his first wife, and altogether he had fathered twenty children, twelve of whom survived to adulthood. He taught them that slavery was an offense to God. Five sons had already moved to Kansas to fight for the abolitionist cause. Back East the Browns had been active in the Underground Railroad, and in Kansas they immediately started helping slaves escape to Canada. It would soon become clear that John Brown and his sons would stop at nothing to achieve their goal of freeing the slaves. In Bleeding Kansas they would be responsible for some of the bloodiest violence of all.

After a few days in Lawrence, Isaac decided it was safe for him and Billy to go home. He stayed at the farm for a short visit and then said good-bye to Billy and the rest of the family and returned to Grasshopper Falls.

Billy found work caring for the livestock of free-state neighbors. Even the very small wages he earned were helpful. Because of on-going drought, the corn crop had been so poor that every settler in the valley was suffering. "We had now been reduced to utter destitution," Billy said.

Isaac's tormentors were still at it. According to Billy, "hardly a day passed without some of them inquiring 'where the old man was,' saying they would kill him on sight." In spite of these threats, Isaac was even more active in politics. He visited Robinson, Lane, and Brown, and they in turn visited him in Grasshopper Falls. They also came to the family home in the Salt Creek Valley, being careful not to draw attention to themselves.

By the end of 1855, Kansas had a newly appointed governor, Wilson Shannon, the former governor of Ohio. Although Shannon was a Southern sympathizer, he tried to govern the unruly territory in a way that would protect the most citizens. He later wrote of this period, "Govern Kansas! You might as well attempt to govern the devil in hell."

He requested that the federal government station troops in Kansas to keep the peace. When this was denied, he asked for volunteers to form a Kansas militia, and nearly 1,200 mostly pro-slave men responded. Their first task was to arrest several free-staters in Lawrence who had broken the law. As the militia gathered a few miles away to storm the town, the Lawrence militia prepared for the attack. Free-state men from all over the area rushed to help, including John Brown and his sons.

The siege of Lawrence began on December 1, 1855. Governor Shannon pleaded again for assistance from federal troops, but the US government still did not want to get involved in "local" squabbles. Using all his political finesse, the desperate governor managed to negotiate the Treaty of Lawrence on December 10, narrowly averting an all-out battle. He was assisted by a spell of freezing weather that took the fight out of both sides. When the crisis was over, Shannon warned President Pierce that the violence between the abolitionists and the pro-slave forces would have national ramifications.

The event wasn't given much importance outside Kansas. Had people paid attention, they would have realized that what was happening in Kansas was a foreshadowing of what would soon consume the entire nation.

CHAPTER 11

JOHN BROWN'S WAR IN KANSAS

◆—◆—◆

The hard times for Billy and his family were about to get worse. In January 1856, a month before Billy turned ten, Isaac declared himself a candidate for the Free State legislature. Pro-slavers in Leavenworth threatened to kill anyone who dared to vote, so the Lawrence militia traveled the thirty-five miles to protect voters at a polling site there. The following day pro-slavers ambushed and killed the leader of the militia. But the elections went forward. When the votes were tallied, Isaac was declared one of the Free State Party's sixty new legislators.

Billy knew that his father was now even more at risk, but he admired his bravery for attending every Free State legislative session in Topeka. Because President Pierce sympathized with the South, he ignored this new legislative body and continued to recognize the pro-slave legislature as the territory's legitimate government. He also recognized the pro-slave village of Lecompton, just twelve miles from Lawrence, as the territorial capital.

That spring, Sheriff Jones, a pro-slaver whose jurisdiction included Lawrence, was shot in the back by an unknown assailant. He survived, and, certain that free-staters were responsible, he wanted revenge. Sympathetic federal officials authorized him to arrest Charles Robinson and Jim Lane, the abolitionist leaders. The sheriff headed to Lawrence on May 21 with a posse of seven hundred border ruffians who dragged along five cannons.

Robinson and Lane had been forewarned and had left town. Knowing this, residents gambled that the posse would not make trouble, and they offered no resistance. When Sheriff Jones couldn't find Robinson and Lane, he exploded in anger and gave his men permission to pillage

Lawrence had a population of 1,500 people—almost all of them opposed to slavery—when Sheriff Jones and his posse of border ruffians attacked it.

the town. The townspeople tried to resist, but they were quickly overwhelmed. Businesses were destroyed and homes were looted and burned. The Free State Hotel that had so impressed Billy during his visit to Lawrence was blown up with gunpowder. An eyewitness later claimed that "as the flames hissed and crackled, the sheriff leaned upon his horse and contemplated the spectacle. His eyes glistened with a wild delight, and he said, 'This is the happiest moment of my life.'"

Because the Free State Hotel, the pride of Lawrence, was the headquarters of the abolitionists, Sheriff Jones ordered it to be destroyed.

John Brown and his sons arrived too late to help. Looking over the smoldering ruins, Brown vowed revenge. What happened on the floor of the Senate in Washington, DC, the next day enraged him further. When a Massachusetts senator denounced Southerners for their support of pro-slavers in Kansas, a South Carolina senator physically attacked him, injuring him severely.

Two days later, on the evening of May 24, John Brown's men approached several cabins near Pottawatomie Creek in Kansas. The pro-slave occupants had not been involved in the sacking of Lawrence, nor did they own slaves. But Brown apparently believed they might be involved in a plan to attack his family. He had five unarmed men dragged from their beds and killed them in front of their families.

John Brown's radical actions in executing several pro-slave settlers helped ignite all-out violence in Kansas.

This incident, called the Pottawatomie Massacre, signaled the beginning of heavy guerrilla warfare in Kansas. Money and weapons poured in from other parts of the country to support both sides. Pro-slavers were greater in number, but free-staters were better armed. Mayhem reigned as free-staters and pro-slavers murdered each other, and pillaged and burned one another's communities. President Pierce finally paid attention to Kansas and sent federal troops, but even they had little success in restoring order.

Newspapers from all over the country sent reporters to cover the violence, and Kansas became front-page news. In New York City, Horace Greeley, the influential editor of the *New York Tribune* newspaper, coined the term "Bleeding Kansas" to describe what was happening. Greeley, who opposed slavery, had been the first to call the Missouri pro-slave raiders "border ruffians."

Nobody was safe. Ten-year-old Billy had gone to Fort Leavenworth on an errand for his mother and was riding home in the company of two free-state men. As the three crossed a stream, bullets suddenly whizzed around them. Before they could take shelter, one of the men was struck and killed. Billy said that he and the other man "put spurs to our horses and made a dash for our lives."

A girl whose abolitionist family was continually threatened never forgot the fear they all felt during this time. "Those were heart-rending days for my young mother. Many times she answered the door when, if my father had gone, he would have been instantly shot down. He was ordered time and again to leave the place inside of twenty-four hours." When her father went into hiding, "my mother knew not whether he was dead or alive."

John Brown quickly made headlines again. A pro-slave militia of fifty to sixty men had set out for his Osawatomie home to arrest him. Along the way they captured two of his sons, pillaged a couple of villages, and then stopped to camp at a place called Black Jack. When Brown learned about his sons, he was determined to rescue them. He and his men were badly outnumbered, but they fought fiercely. They took two dozen of their enemies captive and used them to barter for the release of Brown's sons and several other prisoners. The pro-slave leader wrote of the Battle of Black Jack, "I went to take Old Brown and he took me."

Governor Shannon resigned in frustration, and the president appointed Daniel Woodson, a pro-slave Virginian, to be the acting governor. President Pierce also ordered federal troops to break up the Free State legislature meeting in Topeka. At the same time, a bill to admit Kansas to the Union as a free state passed the US House, but was rejected by the Senate. When Billy heard about it, he wondered if Kansas would ever become a state.

During all this, the Underground Railroad was active. John Brown personally helped many slaves to freedom. On one trip he and a group of slaves were overtaken by slave hunters. A skilled fighter, Brown got the better of them and took them prisoner. Before releasing them, the deeply religious Brown forced them at gunpoint to kneel and pray for their sins.

A Kansas pioneer woman whose home was a stop on the Underground Railroad recalled that John Brown came by regularly. The last time, she said, he arrived at her family's cabin late at night in a covered wagon carrying sixteen slaves. The next morning, "before they left, my mother and I got up and cooked their breakfast . . . I remember they all sat down at a long table with John Brown at the head. A little baby had been born on the way, and they had christened him John Brown."

CHAPTER 12

FATHER

❖

The spring of 1856 was not a good one for Billy, his family, or Kansas. The conflict grew worse every day. "Men were shot down in their homes, around their firesides, in the furrows behind the plow—everywhere," Billy said. "Widows and orphans multiplied . . . while the incendiary torch lit up the prairie heavens."

Plundering, looting, and burning were common when the violence in Kansas was at its worst. This drawing shows mayhem in Lawrence.

For pro-slavers, John Brown was the prize. He was the most dangerous of the abolitionists and also had a price on his head. Early on an August morning in 1856, a militia of three hundred pro-slave men on horseback thundered toward Brown's home in Osawatomie, determined that this time they would silence him. Their scouting party approached the outskirts of the free-state village just as dawn was breaking and saw Brown's son Frederick, age twenty-six, outside a friend's home. Frederick greeted them, not knowing who they were. But the leader knew who Frederick was. He drew his gun, killing Frederick instantly.

Neighbors raised the alarm. A thirteen-year-old boy raced to the village to warn the residents. John Brown quickly gathered his own militia of fifty men to defend Osawatomie. He decided to confront the raiders before they reached the village, hoping to

spare the townspeople from the violence. Brown and his men fought hard but were badly outnumbered and finally had to flee.

Homegrown militias sprang up all over the area, with both sides continually challenging each other and sometimes setting up ambushes.

The pro-slave force ransacked and burned nearly forty homes in Osawatomie. According to an eyewitness, "After taking every horse and wagon and loading them with stolen goods and their own dead and wounded, they left town by the same route over which they came. They stopped at the first house west of town and plundered and burned it. The [owner] had a fine piano, the first and only one in the vicinity. This the ruffians tried desperately to load, but they abandoned the project and it was burned with the other contents of the house."

At another cabin, women and children were huddled together after their men had fled to the woods. A young mother later wrote that the children started screaming when the pro-slavers arrived. One of the men shouted out, "'We will not kill women and children, but if we get hold of any men, we'll put this over their heads mighty quick,' and he shook out a rope. They then departed, taking with them [our] cows and calves."

As a defeated John Brown watched the village of Osawatomie burn, he tried to absorb the loss of his son Frederick. He told his son Jason, "I have only a short time to live—only one death to die, and I will die fighting for this cause. There will be no more peace in this land until slavery is done for."

Brown's stand that day in defending Osawatomie against overwhelming odds made him an abolitionist hero. After that, he was often called Osawatomie Brown.

Soon President Pierce appointed another new governor—John White Geary, a military man from Pennsylvania. Billy and his family felt heartened when he disbanded all local militia groups and used federal troops to control bands of border ruffians. Still, these ruffians managed to plunder and burn Grasshopper Falls. Isaac was not there, but he knew they had wanted to find and kill him. He and Mary decided that he had to leave the area for a while. His old wound was troubling him. He needed somewhere safe to recover.

Once more the family said their sad good-byes. "With the help of John Brown, Jim Lane, and other free-soilers, father made his way back to Ohio," Billy said. He reached Cleveland safely and recuperated at the home of his brother Joseph. When he felt well enough, the two of them went to a political meeting in Chicago where they met an Illinois politician named Abraham Lincoln. According to Julia, Isaac "addressed the delegates on the subject of 'Bleeding Kansas' and stirred them with his graphic description of the ordeal of terror which the anti-slavery men in that area were undergoing." Whenever Isaac could, he recruited abolitionists to move to Grasshopper Falls to help rebuild it and to fight for the cause of a free Kansas.

While he was gone the family had another brush with danger. A friend came to visit for a few days. Pro-slavers still kept watch on the house, and they mistook the young man for Isaac. During the night the family was awakened by noise outside. "We looked out," said Billy, "and saw that the house was surrounded by a party of men."

The children were frightened, but Mary Cody remained calm. "Opening a window, she [called] out in a firm tone of voice, 'Who are you? What do you want here?'" Billy later recalled.

"'We are after that old abolitionist husband of yours,' came the answer.

"'He is not in this house, and has not been here for a long time,' said my mother.

"'That's a lie! We know he is in the house, and we are bound to have him,' said the spokesman of the party.

"'My husband is not at home,' emphatically repeated my heroic mother—for if there ever was a heroine she certainly was one—'but the house is full of armed men . . . and I'll give you just two minutes to get out of the yard; if you're not out by the end of that time, I shall order them to fire on you.'"

Mary instructed their visitor to sound like an officer and shout out orders. Hearing him, the men outside "supposed that my mother really had quite a force at her command. Then she stepped to the open window again and said, 'You and your friends had better go away or the men will surely fire on you.'"

All those inside stamped their feet so they sounded like soldiers lining up and preparing to fire. It worked. "The cowardly villains began retreating, and then my mother fired an old gun into the air which greatly accelerated their speed, causing them to break and run. They soon disappeared from view in the darkness," Billy said.

"The next morning we discovered that they had intended to blow up the house. We found two kegs of powder together with a fuse. It only required a lighted match to have sent us into eternity. My mother's presence of mind, which had never yet deserted her in any trying situation, had saved our lives."

Isaac came home just before Christmas, his health greatly improved. He shared with his family his experiences in Ohio, and he was eager to know everything that had happened in the Salt Creek Valley. Julia said the next month was "a joyous time. With father home once again, Christmas was a happy occasion with extra-special gifts under the tree, sent by Joseph Cody and his family."

Early in the new year of 1857, Isaac went back to Ohio to guide the families he'd recruited in their move to Grasshopper Falls. By then Billy had turned eleven, and he anxiously awaited his father's homecoming.

Isaac returned to his family in the spring. With him was a group of emigrant families who planned to camp in the Codys' yard for a few days before locating their claims. Then scarlet fever broke out among them. Highly infectious and with no known treatment, it quickly spread. Several people died.

According to Julia, everyone in the family helped all they could. They also assisted in burying the dead. Isaac had urged these people to come to Kansas and felt responsible for what had happened.

"Though worn by work and worry," Julia said, "he labored day and night to see that the fever did not spread and to aid those who had fallen prey to the disease."

Isaac was exhausted. He did not catch scarlet fever, but he fell ill with a cold that soon turned into pneumonia, complicated by his old injury. Mary Cody sent an urgent message to Elijah, and he brought the doctor from Weston to tend to Isaac. But the doctor shook his head and said there was no hope. Billy could do nothing but hold a vigil at his beloved father's bedside. Just before dawn on April 27, surrounded by his family, Isaac died.

"The wound inflicted by Dunn had at last fulfilled the murderer's purpose," Billy said.

Elijah assisted with funeral arrangements, and Isaac was buried in the Leavenworth cemetery. Somehow the family had to go on without the husband and father they loved so much.

They had lost Samuel four years ago. Now Father was gone. Billy wasn't sure they could survive this new loss.

Billy was eleven when his father died, three years after he was stabbed by a pro-slaver.

85

BILLY THE HERO

◆•◆•◆

Even as Billy grieved for his father, he had to assume a new role once again. He could no longer merely contribute to supporting his mother, five sisters, and little brother. He had to do more. "I was eleven years old, and the only man of the family. I made up my mind to be the breadwinner."

Farming held no appeal for him. Everything he dreamed of was out West: "I determined to follow the plains for a livelihood for them and myself." But for now, his mother needed him at home. He found a job herding cattle for a neighbor and earned fifty cents a day, but that was barely enough to help his mother with expenses.

Soon the family had a new worry. "At this sorrowful period, Mother was almost at death's door with consumption," reported Helen. Now called tuberculosis, the disease attacks the lungs and slowly weakens its victim. The children were frantic with the fear of losing their mother. But Mary Cody rallied, and the crisis passed.

She would need all her strength to deal with yet another challenge. A pro-slave businessman brought charges against her, claiming that Isaac owed him a thousand dollars for lumber and supplies. Mary knew that her husband had paid his debt, but he had neglected to get a receipt. The only eyewitness who could testify on Isaac's behalf had disappeared.

Mary turned to Elijah to intercede on her behalf—but Elijah failed her, siding with the businessman because of their shared politics. That he would choose party loyalty over his dead brother's family was too much for Mary, and she broke off contact with him. Shortly after, Elijah left Missouri.

Without Elijah's help, Mary Cody needed to hire a lawyer. If she lost the case, she would have to sell the farm to pay the bill. Desperate to help save his family's home, Billy talked his mother into going with him to the headquarters of Russell, Majors & Waddell in Leavenworth to see if they would employ him again. Billy told Alexander Majors that he had promised his father he would support the family—it was his responsibility as the eldest son. Majors offered him a job as a messenger boy at twenty-five dollars a month—the same wage he had earned herding cattle for the company, and double what he was making working for the neighbors. Because Billy would still live at home, his mother gave her approval.

The freight company issued him a mule, and for the next two months Billy carried messages between the freight offices and the

Mary Cody agreed to go with Billy to Leavenworth so he could ask for a job.

telegraph station at Fort Leavenworth. He earned enough that his mother was able to hire a young lawyer to take her case. At the last moment, the eyewitness showed up. He testified that he saw Isaac Cody pay his bill in full. The family home was saved.

With that crisis averted and his mother's health improving, Billy thought hard about his future. His mother had rented out the farm's fields to neighboring farmers, and she was taking in boarders at the house—an enterprise Billy's sisters helped with—but it still wasn't enough. How, Billy wondered, could he increase his earnings and also see the West of his dreams?

Then he learned that his employers had received a major government contract to supply goods and fresh meat to the US Army in Utah, where they were in a standoff with the Mormons. Huge convoys of wagon trains and cattle would soon be heading west, with each trip lasting several months. The pay was good. Billy wanted to go.

Using all his charm, he persuaded Russell and Majors to hire him to help with the cattle that would trail behind the wagon train. This was a grown man's work, and they agreed to pay him full wages—forty dollars a month—which he instructed them to hand directly to his mother. "With forty dollars a month she would be able to support [my sisters] and baby brother in comfort," Billy said.

Mary Cody gave her reluctant consent. In late June she and Billy's sisters helped him get ready. Helen later described the moment when Billy left, noting that it was a difficult ordeal for their mother, especially since hostile native tribes were a real threat to anyone crossing land they considered to be their own. "With tears in our eyes we crowded about him, imploring him to run if he saw any Indians," Helen said. This advice would prove prophetic.

The wagon train journeyed north into Nebraska Territory to follow the Platte River toward Fort Kearny. Billy missed his family but loved life on the trail. The work required him to use his riding and roping skills and to be outside in any kind of weather. Through long days Billy helped keep the cattle plodding along. At night he slept under the stars, his saddlebag serving as his pillow and his rifle within reach in case of attack.

"The trip [was] full of excitement for me," Billy said. "Camp life was rough, the bacon often rusty and the flour moldy, but the hard work gave us big appetites. Plainsmen learn not to be particular."

All went well until they neared Fort Kearny. The cattle were slow, and Billy and the other fourteen herders had fallen behind the

Herders worked from early light until dark. They averaged about fifteen miles a day on the trail. If they moved any faster, the cattle grew too thin.

wagon train. When they stopped for lunch at Plum Creek in Nebraska Territory, three herders kept watch on the cattle as the others ate. Then suddenly, Billy said, "there was a sharp Bang! Bang! Bang! And the thunder of hoofs."

Billy grabbed his rifle as the trail boss cried out, "Indians! They've shot two herders and stampeded the cattle!" The herders were killed outright. The third, shot in the leg, managed to stumble to camp. Billy realized that he and the dozen other herders were badly outnumbered. Following orders from the trail boss, everyone ran toward the creek, half dragging the injured man. They all jumped over the bank, huddling under the overhanging ledge for cover.

They waited with their pistols and rifles cocked and ready, but nothing happened. When it grew dark, the herders debated what to do. No one wanted to climb up the riverbank and find out if the Indians were waiting for them. Instead they decided to follow Plum Creek until it met the wide, shallow Platte River. Under the cover of darkness they could walk in the riverbed where the water was shallow and swim where it deepened until they reached Fort Kearny, still thirty miles away.

They built a primitive raft of tree branches for the injured man and set out. When they reached the Platte, they trudged and swam through the river, pulling the raft. Eleven-year-old Billy was the youngest and smallest of the herders, and in several places the water was as high as his shoulders.

"It was a long [exhausting] journey, but our lives depended on keeping along the river bed," Billy said. "Gradually I fell behind . . . dragging one weary step after another." Then, in the light of the rising moon, Billy saw an Indian warrior at the top of the riverbank aiming his rifle at one of the men up ahead. Billy reacted instantly. "I knew well enough that in another second he would drop one of my friends. So I raised my rifle and fired."

He saw the man fall headlong into the river. "I was not only overcome with astonishment, but was badly scared, as I could hardly realize what I had done." The men came running when they heard the shot. Afraid it had alerted the Indians to their location, they all scrambled on down the river. In spite of their hunger and exhaustion, "we pushed on . . . toward Fort Kearny, which we reached about daylight," Billy said, relieved to be safe at last. "We were given food and sent to bed while the soldiers set out to look for our slain comrades and try to recover our cattle." They found the two dead herders' bodies, but the cattle were lost.

Billy and the other herders caught rides back to Leavenworth on returning freight wagons. When Billy reached town he was interviewed by the editor of the local newspaper, who had heard what he'd done. When the story was published, "it made me the envy of all the boys," Billy said. "I felt very much elated over this. . . . Again

and again I read with eager interest the long and sensational account of our adventure. My exploit was related in a very graphic
manner, and for a long time afterwards I was considered a hero."

His fourteen-year-old sister Julia had a different reaction. She
thought her brother was too full of himself. "Billy walked around
for days with his head high in the air," she reported.

Along with the rest of the family, she was appalled by how
dirty he was—though it was understandable, since trail hands had
few opportunities to wash themselves or their clothes. "[Mother]
rushed Billy off to the bathroom where he soon was soaking luxuri-
ously in warm soapy water," Julia said. "Then he dressed in clean
fresh clothes, [while I] gingerly carried the old ones to the stove
and burned them, and then he joined the family at supper. The
roast beef, vegetables, apple pie and milk constituted a magnificent
feast compared to his recent steady diet of hardtack, fat pork and
black coffee."

CHAPTER 14

TROUBLE WITH THE MORMONS

B illy's wagon train adventures cemented his longing to "lead a life on the plains." But his mother refused to discuss this possibility. The family was grieving the sudden death of Billy's oldest sister, Martha—Isaac's daughter from his previous marriage—who had caught a mysterious illness. Mary Cody wasn't about to let another of her children knowingly risk danger. Billy was safer at home, she argued. Since Isaac's death, the pro-slavers had at long last ceased tormenting the family. Eastern Kansas was less violent now. Not only was it occupied by federal troops, but, just as important, John Brown had left the state to go back East. Mary Cody wanted Billy to find work close to home and return to school. He was, after all, only eleven.

So Billy did odd jobs for the freight company to earn a little money, and he also went to school—never his favorite thing.

Money troubles continued to shadow the Cody household. Mary's tuberculosis treatments were expensive, and the family was in debt. Since women and girls had few options for employment outside the home, Billy was their best hope for income. He begged to be allowed to go back on the trail, arguing that he could make the most money there—and it was where he longed to be. Finally his mother relented, and once again Billy convinced his employers at the freight company to send him out West. Alexander Majors signed him up for the next wagon train to Utah at his old salary of forty dollars a month. "You seem to have a reputation as a frontiersman, Billy," he told the boy.

The West was a dangerous place that fall of 1857, and hostile natives were only one reason. Anyone entering Utah Territory had to beware of Mormons.

The Mormon religion, known as the Church of Jesus Christ of Latter-Day Saints, was founded in New York State by Joseph Smith in 1830. According to Smith, he and his followers had a divine right to establish their own kingdom. Wherever they settled, they bought up land that would then be owned by the Mormon church. Locals were alarmed, worried that they were being pushed aside and would lose their homes and businesses. They also objected to the Mormon practice of polygamy, which allowed a man to have more than one wife. The Mormons' growing power led to violence on both sides and to the Mormons' being driven out of several places.

Smith wanted his followers to be free of harassment, and he began plans to relocate the Mormons out West in a place where they could live apart from mainstream society. He did not live to see this become reality, for he was murdered by an anti-Mormon mob in Illinois in 1844. But his successor, Brigham Young, pushed this plan forward. Church leaders selected Utah's Valley of the Great Salt Lake. Mormons started the overland trek, mapping out what became known as the Mormon Trail, which ran along the north side of the Platte River, opposite the Oregon Trail on the south side. Eventually seventy thousand Mormons, including Young, migrated to Utah.

In an attempt to avoid hostilities with the Mormons, the US government appointed Young the governor of Utah Territory. But Young was often uncooperative, intent that the Mormon kingdom would be independent of the federal government. If it took violence to keep all others away, so be it.

In 1857, at a place called Mountain Meadows, a small group

of Mormons massacred a party of 120 pioneers crossing southern Utah on their way to California. Exactly who ordered the massacre or why isn't known, but the US government responded by ordering the army to Salt Lake City to depose Young and install a governor selected by the newly elected president, James Buchanan.

Both the government and the Mormons were clear about their goals. "'We do not want to fight the United States,' declared Young, 'but if they drive us to it, we shall do the best we can; and I will tell you, as the Lord liveth we shall come off conquerors.'" Anyone, military or otherwise, heading into the Salt Lake Valley could expect trouble from Mormon vigilantes.

The first army commander appointed to confront Young felt just as strongly in his convictions as the Mormons, saying, "I am ordered there, and I will winter in the Valley of the Salt Lake—or in Hell."

None of that worried Billy, who was assigned to one of the wagon trains that followed behind the army with supplies. "Our long train, twenty-five wagons, each with its six yoke of oxen, rolled slowly out of Leavenworth over the western trail. . . . It was an impressive sight. This was to be a long journey, clear to the Utah country, and I eagerly looked forward to new adventures."

Depending on the weather, such a trip took at least three months, for Salt Lake City was 1,100 miles from Leavenworth, Kansas.

Billy's trail boss, Lew Simpson, was an experienced frontiersman. Billy greatly admired him. During evenings around the campfire Billy would listen to the men tell their tall tales, and no one could outdo Simpson, who loved to exaggerate feats of roping, riding, and fighting Indians. Billy also admired twenty-one-year-old James Butler Hickok, called "Wild Bill" by everyone because of his exploits on the trail. He had killed a bear with a bowie knife and was an excellent marksman. He was also a natural leader with a strong sense of right and wrong. All the men respected him.

Billy's main assignment was to help with the cattle, but he was interested in learning to be a wagon driver so he'd have that skill if he ever needed it. Whenever he had the opportunity, he climbed up next to the bullwhackers who drove the wagons. Sometimes he got to take over for a little while. Each wagon and its contents

This wagon train traveled from Leavenworth to Denver. Wagon trains often encountered such dangers as bad weather, contagious disease, and hostile Indians and outlaws.

Herders always looked forward to mealtime. Their diet was mostly meat, beans, and bread. Usually the cook also served as handyman, doctor, barber, and clothes-mender.

weighed up to seven thousand pounds, so to keep the oxen moving at a steady pace required considerable skill.

Billy got along with everyone except one man who, he said, "took particular delight in bullying and tyrannizing me." One time, Billy recalled, when everyone was eating, he ordered Billy to run an errand for him, and when Billy didn't immediately move to do it, "he gave me a slap in the face with the back of his hand, knocking me off an ox-yoke on which I was sitting and sending me sprawling on the ground." Billy grabbed a pot of hot coffee and threw it at the bully, enraging him so much that he "would undoubtedly have torn me to pieces, had it not been for the timely interference of my new-found friend, Wild Bill, who knocked the man down."

Wild Bill then warned him, "If you ever again lay a hand on that boy, I'll give you such a pounding that you won't get over it for a month of Sundays." Billy glowed with pleasure. He recalled that in spite of the ten-year age difference between the two, "from that time forward, Wild Bill was my protector and friend."

Over the next weeks, Billy experienced some of the very real dangers of an overland trip. A buffalo stampede damaged many of the wagons. That was followed just days later by two Indian attacks. "We beat off the attacks, but lost two men," Billy reported.

They had no further problems until, only a hundred miles from Salt Lake City, they stopped one day near a creek to water the cattle. Suddenly they were surrounded by twenty men on horseback.

Billy looked around. "They were all armed with double-barreled shotguns, rifles and revolvers . . . and had covered us with their weapons, so that we were completely at their mercy."

"'I'll trouble you for your six-shooters, gentlemen,' said the leader, a big, bearded man.

"'I'll give 'em to you in a way you don't want,' replied Simpson.

"The next moment three guns were leveled at Simpson. 'If you make a move you're a dead man,' said the leader."

Billy and the others put their hands in the air. "Simpson was a brave man, but the strangers had the drop. At the same time, we saw that the wagons were surrounded by several hundred men, all mounted and armed. . . . We knew that we had fallen into the hands of the Mormon Danites, or Destroying Angels. . . . The leader was Lott Smith, one of the bravest and most determined of the whole crowd."

Billy probably mislabeled the men as Danites—a group of violent Mormon vigilantes who may not have been operative at that time. Instead, the men were probably Brigham Young's Territorial Militia. Either way, according to Billy, Smith directed his men to take all the provisions they could carry and then burn the wagons. Then Smith told Billy and the other thirty herders that he didn't intend to kill them, provided they did what they were told. When he informed Simpson that they could keep only one supply wagon and team of oxen, along with enough food to see them the hundred miles back to Fort Bridger, Wyoming, Simpson dared to protest that they needed their guns in case they encountered hostile Indians.

Billy held his breath as he watched the tense negotiation. Finally Smith agreed to let the men keep their guns, but he told them he was taking their horses. As the herders set out on foot, Smith had one more message for them: they would be shot if they tried to turn back. "They watched us depart," Billy said. "When we had moved a little way off, we saw a blaze against the sky behind us, and knew that our wagon train had been fired." It was a frightening moment for Billy and the herders. "The smoke [rolled] up in dense clouds. Some of the wagons were loaded with ammunition, and it was not long before loud explosions followed in rapid succession."

Luckily, the Indians left the group alone as they trudged the hundred miles alongside their one supply wagon. All the men kept a close eye on the weather, concerned that if they got caught up in freezing rain, it would add more misery to an already difficult journey. Even worse, if they got hit with an early season blizzard, it could delay them so long that they would run out of food. Finally, a week after setting out, they reached Fort Bridger and learned that two other Russell, Majors & Waddell wagon trains had met the same fate. It was now late November, and four hundred employees of the company, including Billy and Wild Bill Hickok, were stranded at the fort for the winter.

That February Billy turned twelve. A cavalry trooper who got to know him during those long winter months at the fort later wrote that Billy "impressed me as a rather fresh, 'smart-elick' sort of kid. The bullwhackers had made quite a pet of him and one of them informed me that Billy was already developing won-derful skill at riding wild horses or mules, shooting and throwing a rope."

This 1861 military map includes places Billy visited during the time he worked on the trails, including Fort Bridger, Wyoming, where he and other herders took refuge.

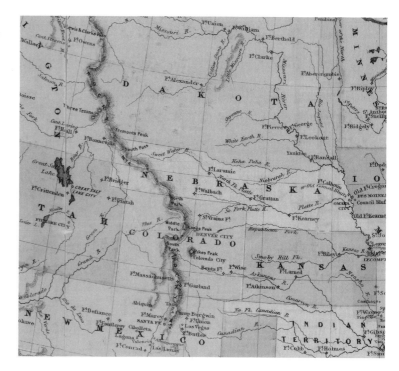

But conditions at the fort were severe. Mormon vigilantes cut off supply trails, and the men's daily ration of food grew smaller and smaller. Temperatures hit thirty degrees below zero for days at a time. Every day the men scavenged the surrounding area for wood and sagebrush to burn for warmth.

Finally a late spring thaw allowed Billy and the others to form groups and start for Kansas. Billy's group stopped at Fort Laramie, Wyoming, on the way and had their first real meal in months. Billy thought that the hardtack, bacon, beans, and coffee they were served was one of the best meals he'd ever eaten.

When he finally arrived home in the middle of the summer of

1858, seven months after he'd left, he said, "The first to welcome me was my old dog Turk, who came tearing toward me and almost knocked me down in his eagerness. I am sure my mother and sisters and little brother were mighty glad to see me. They had feared that I might never return."

CHAPTER 15

BILLY AND THE INDIANS

◆ ◆ ◆

Wild Bill Hickok came home with Billy. Sixteen-year-old Julia was immediately smitten, describing Wild Bill as having eyes of pure blue and long, light blond hair that "fell in ringlets over his shoulders." In spite of his tough reputation, she found this tall, handsome plainsman to be "gentle, soft-spoken, considerate and kind."

Wild Bill was known for his quick shot and iron nerves. His occupations included cowhand, gunfighter, lawman, soldier, and actor. He was also a gambler and was killed at age thirty-nine while playing poker.

Wild Bill was equally smitten by Billy's pretty brown-eyed sister. When Wild Bill asked Julia to marry him, she was both pleased and flattered. But she thought she'd better consult Billy as to whether Wild Bill would make a good husband. "'Julia,' Billy said, 'Wild Bill is my best friend and a man among men. But he loves the plains, he lives for adventure, and even though he'd try with all his might, he could never settle down. Marrying Bill Hickok and trying to house-break him would be harder than saddling a grizzly bear.'"

Julia knew that Billy was right, and she turned down Wild Bill's proposal. However, she remained good friends with him. He visited the Cody farm whenever he could and was always warmly welcomed. According to Julia, he "always referred to the Salt Creek Valley house as his home."

Twelve-year-old Billy stayed with his family for the rest of the summer of 1858. He helped with the chores, did jobs in town for the freight company, and once again went back to school. By early fall he felt stir-crazy. Mary Cody saw it. When Billy's bosses of-fered him a job with a supply train headed to Fort Laramie, she consented, though it was hard for her to have him leave. Because her tuberculosis was getting worse, she always worried that each departure would be the last time she would see him.

Everything went smoothly on the seven-hundred-mile trip to Fort Laramie. Traveling twelve to fifteen miles a day, Billy and the supply train reached the Wyoming fort in early November. Winter weather prevented them from leaving for a while, so Billy settled in and enjoyed his surroundings.

If he had to be stranded somewhere, Fort Laramie was a good place. It was a busy frontier fort as well as a huge trading post. Every traveler crossing the country on the Oregon Trail or the Mormon Trail stopped there. For those going west, it was the gateway to the Rocky Mountains. For those returning, the sight of the fort's uniformed soldiers and the American flag flying in the breeze gave welcome comfort.

Several thousand Indians—most of them Sioux, Northern Cheyenne, and Northern Arapaho—traded regu-

This 1871 photo shows a Northern Cheyenne village at Fort Laramie. Billy was always fascinated by Native Americans and their culture.

larly at the fort and had their camps nearby. According to Billy, Fort Laramie "had become the most famous meeting-place of the plains. Here the greatest Indian councils were held, and here also came the most celebrated of the Indian fighters, men whose names had long been known to me, but whom I never dared hope to see." Among them were Jim Bridger, for whom Fort Bridger was named, and Kit Carson, the famed hunter, trapper, and Indian fighter. Billy described him as "a small, dapper, quiet man whom everybody held in profound respect."

Kit Carson fascinated Billy. "I used to sit for hours and watch him and the others talk to the Indians in sign language. Without a sound they would carry on long and interesting conversations, tell stories, inquire about game and trails, and discuss pretty much everything that men find worth discussing."

Of the thirty Plains Indian tribes, the major ones were the Sioux, Blackfoot, Cheyenne, Comanche, Crow, and Kiowa. Since each tribe had its own language, the Plains Indians had developed a sign language to communicate among the tribes. Sign language was also useful for communicating with non-Indians like Billy. Within tribes it was put to good use when Indians needed to communicate during ambushes. Billy set to work and learned it quickly. "I . . . began my education in it with far more interest than I had given to the 'three R's' back at Salt Creek."

He also found time to play. "My wagon bed became [a] splendid playhouse for the Indian children from the villages. . . . I joined them in their games, and from them picked up a fair working knowledge of the Sioux language."

Finally, in January 1859, Billy left the fort on an eastbound wagon train. He arrived home just after his thirteenth birthday in February. Because his mother insisted, he returned to school and stuck with his lessons. By spring he could stand it no more and joined a group of Kansas men headed to Colorado to prospect for gold. By fall, he was back home, the venture having failed.

His mother's health was declining, which made Billy uneasy about signing on to another long-term commitment with a wagon train. Instead, he teamed up with Dave Harrington, an experienced trapper ten years his senior, to go into the fur business. With a wagon and two oxen they set out for central Kansas in search of otter and beaver pelts.

Two hundred miles from the Salt Creek Valley they found an area rich with otter and beaver. They built a dugout in the side of a hill and set their traps, quickly accumulating over three hundred pelts. But bad luck struck. One of the oxen died in a fall, and the other was killed by a bear. Then, while tracking an elk, Billy lost his balance on a slippery stone in a creek bed. "Snap! went something," Billy later recalled, "and looking down I saw my foot hanging useless. I had broken my leg just above the ankle. . . . I was very miserable when Harington came up. I urged him to shoot me, but he laughingly replied that that would hardly do."

Luckily, Harington knew enough about such injuries to properly set Billy's leg. They decided Harrington must go get help and estimated that he would be gone twenty days. He got Billy settled into the dugout with enough food and plenty of blankets. "I watched him start off on foot, and my heart was heavy," Billy said. "But soon

I stopped thinking of my pain and began to find ways and means to cure my loneliness. We had brought with us a number of books and these I read through most of my waking hours."

Heavy snow fell and the days dragged by. Billy cut a notch on a stick for each one. "I had cut twelve of these notches when one morning I was awakened from a sound sleep by the touch of a hand on my shoulder." Billy was instantly alert, his heart pounding as he looked into the painted face of a Sioux warrior. "The brilliant colors that had been smeared on his visage told me more forcibly than words . . . that his tribe was on the warpath. It was a decidedly unpleasant discovery for me."

Warriors crowded into the dugout. Billy heard others outside. He might be only thirteen, but he knew that wouldn't stop them from killing him. One of the warriors made his way to Billy's side. "It was plain from the deference accorded him by the others that he was a chief. As soon as I set eyes on him, I recognized him as . . . Rain-in-the-Face, whom I had often seen and talked with at Fort Laramie, and whose children taught me the Sioux language as we played together."

Billy respectfully addressed the chief by name. He showed him his leg and asked in the Sioux language if the chief remembered him. "He replied that he did. I asked him if he intended to kill the boy who had been his children's playmate. He consulted with his warriors, who had begun busily to loot the dugout. After a long

Thirteen-year-old Billy's knowledge of the Sioux language helped him talk his way out of danger when Sioux warriors discovered him in the cave.

parley [he] told me that my life would be spared, but my gun and pistol and all my provisions would be regarded as the spoils of war."

Billy was not yet out of danger. Although the Indians did not discover the stash of fur pelts hidden outside, they stole almost everything else, leaving only some deer meat. With his matches all gone, Billy did not dare let his small fire go out and forced himself to sleep in snatches so he could keep it going. The pain in his leg when he hobbled to the woodpile was excruciating, but he knew that his life depended on the fire, for it provided heat, light, and a way to cook the deer meat. Wolves smelled the meat and howled outside the dugout at night, pawing and scratching to get in.

It snowed every day, burying the dugout in heavy drifts. Billy fought off despair. "Worse than all these troubles was the knowledge that the heavy snow would be sure to delay Harrington. . . . How I endured it I do not know. Many and many a time as I lay there I resolved that if I should ever be spared to go back to my home and friends, the frontier should know me no more."

On the twenty-ninth day, "when I had about given up hope, I heard a cheerful voice shouting." Harrington had returned! "He soon cleared a passageway through the snow, and stood beside me. 'I never expected to see you alive again,' he said."

His journey back to the dugout had been treacherous. "Harrington had made a trip few men could have made. All alone he had brought a yoke of oxen over a country where the trails were all obscured and the blinding snow made every added mile more perilous. He had risked his life to save mine."

Unable to walk, Billy rode in the wagon, pulled by the oxen. Along the way he and Harrington stopped to sell their pelts. They made a good profit. It took twenty days to reach the Salt Creek Valley, where Billy's family welcomed him "as one returned from the dead."

He had turned fourteen while he was gone. Grateful that he had survived and that his leg had healed properly, he pledged to stay home to help his mother. But, as before, his vow lasted only a few months. By then, time "had so dulled the memory of my sufferings in the dugout that I had forgotten all about my resolve to forsake the frontier forever." And as he had done time and again, "I looked about me for something new and still more exciting."

CHAPTER 16

BILLY RIDES THE PONY EXPRESS

◆·◆·◆

Billy found something new and exciting in the Pony Express.

In the spring of 1860, Russell, Majors & Waddell launched a grand experiment for delivering mail to the West Coast. Mail from the East could be transported by train to Saint Louis, Missouri, and from there by steamboat to Saint Joseph on the other side of the state. But that was the end of the line unless the mail was sent west by slow-moving stagecoaches—a trip of three weeks or more.

The Pony Express could get mail to the West Coast much faster. Riders carried it all the way from Saint Joseph to Sacramento, California, a distance of nearly two thousand miles, in a mere ten days.

They switched to fresh horses at stations set up every dozen miles or so. Galloping along at a breakneck speed of fifteen miles per hour, each rider covered thirty to forty-five miles before handing over the waterproof mail pouch to a new rider. The route stretched across plains, desert, and two mountain ranges.

One of the advertisements seeking riders stated, "Wanted: Young, skinny, wiry fellows not over 18. Must be expert riders willing to risk death daily. Orphans preferred." The freight company usually sought boys aged sixteen to eighteen. Though Billy was only fourteen,

THE DAILY TIMES.

MONDAY MORNING, JANUARY 30. 1860.

LOCAL AND TERRITORIAL

GREAT EXPRESS ENTERPRISE !

From Leavenworth to Sacramento in Ten Days!

Clear the Track and let the Pony Come Through ?

In our telegraphic columns a few days ago, there was an item stating that it had been decided by the Government to start an Express from the Missouri river to California, and the time to be ten days; but we were not aware that our fellow-citizen, Wm. H. Russell, Esq., was at the head of the enterprise. until we were shown the following di-patch. Its importance can be readily perceived:

The January 30, 1860, issue of the Leavenworth *Daily Times* announced the Pony Express.

115

his old bosses knew him well. He got the job. His pay was over one hundred dollars a month—more than twice what he'd ever made before.

Billy's routes, first in Colorado and then in Wyoming, were physically punishing. He encountered blizzards, sleet and ice, heat waves, hail, mud, and drenching downpours. His mother pleaded with him to quit before he was shaken to death, thrown by his horse, or killed by Indians. But Billy loved every moment of it. Some sources say he was the youngest, lightest, and one of the fastest of the riders, and that one time, discovering that his relief rider had been killed, he completed a distance of 322 miles over rough, dangerous terrain in less than twenty-two hours, changing horses twenty-one times—a record in Pony Express history.

Billy's relief rider was not the only one to be killed. The horses used by the Pony Express were the best to be had, and they were coveted by horse thieves and by Indians, especially those from the Paiute, Shoshone, and Goshute tribes.

Billy had his share of trouble. Once when he was riding an especially fine horse, fifteen Indians chased him. Billy lay flat on the horse's back, knowing that the Indians would avoid hitting the horse with their arrows. He made it to the next station, only to discover that the Indians had already killed the stationmaster and taken the horses. Billy had to gamble that his horse could outrun the Indians' mounts—and it did. When the two of them reached the next station, they had ridden twenty-six miles. That horse had saved Billy's life.

Russell, Majors & Waddell also operated a stage line to the West Coast. Indians had attacked several stagecoaches, killing the passengers and stealing the horses. Eventually both the stage line and Pony Express were so low on horses that they had to shut down. At the time, Billy's old friend Wild Bill was a stagecoach driver, and he invited Billy to join him along with forty other men to try to retrieve some of the horses.

They trailed the thieves into the heart of hostile Indian territory, clear to the Powder River in Wyoming. They could see their horses on the other side of the river. "Never before had [the Indians] been followed so far into their own country," Billy said. "Not dreaming that they would be pursued, they had failed to put out scouts. Wild Bill, who did not know the meaning of fear, made our plan for us."

That night under the cover of darkness, Billy and the others silently crossed the river and crept to the edge of the Indian camp. "At our captain's signal, we rushed pell-mell through their camp. Had we dropped from the clouds, the Indians could not have been more astonished. At the sound of our shots they scattered in every direction, yelling warnings to each other as they fled."

Billy and the men rounded up more than a hundred horses. This number included the Indians' own horses, which the men divided among themselves to keep or sell. According to Billy, the men then celebrated "in the usual manner." For three days they "drank, gambled, and fought . . . with no limit to the rioting and carousing; revelry reigned supreme." Once they were fit to ride again, they delivered the recovered horses to their employers, and the stagecoach line and the Pony Express were back in business.

On one of his rare days off, Billy went on a bear hunt. "I was returning home empty-handed when night overtook me in a lonely spot near a mountain stream. I had killed two sage hens and built a little fire over which to broil them before my night's rest." Suddenly he heard a horse's whinny upstream. Fearing Indians, he went to investigate and found fifteen horses. He looked around and saw light coming from a nearby dugout. He crept close. He could hear men inside talking in English, so he assumed that they were trappers and knocked on the door.

Several moments of silence followed. Then, Billy later recalled, one of the men cried out, "Who's there?"

"'A friend and a white man,' I replied.

"The door opened and a big, ugly-looking fellow stood before me."

Billy was ordered inside. He knew immediately that he was in trouble. "Eight of the most villainous-appearing ruffians I have ever set eyes upon sat about the dugout as I entered. Two of them I recognized at once as teamsters who . . . had been charged with murdering a ranchman and stealing his horses."

Horses were essential for transportation, and Billy knew that horse stealing was big business.

Escape was foremost in Billy's mind. "I was . . . certain that I had uncovered the hiding place of a gang of horse thieves who could have no possible reason to feel anything but hostility toward an honest man."

The men surrounded him. Why was he there? Who else was with him? Billy could see that they were surprised that he was so young. He tried to stay calm and friendly, hoping they would consider him harmless. His biggest worry was that they would take his revolver from him. He told them that he was by himself, camped nearby, and had heard their horses. The leader demanded to know where Billy's horse was. Billy told him it was down the creek. The men wanted to see it—no doubt to steal it before killing him, Billy supposed—and two of the men took him outside. His chance of escape was now or never. When the men started to lead his horse away, Billy made his move. He pulled out his gun and knocked one man unconscious.

"Wheeling about, I saw that the other man, hearing the fall, had turned, his hand upon his revolver. It was no time for argument. I fired and killed him. Then leaping on my horse, I dug the spurs into his sides, and back down the trail we went, over the rocks and rough ground toward safety."

But Billy was not out of danger. The men in the cabin heard the shot and pursued him on foot, "knowing that they could make better time over the rocky country than I could on horseback." As the men gained on him, Billy decided he would have to abandon his horse. "Jumping off, I gave him a smart slap with the butt of my revolver, which sent him down the valley. I turned and began to scramble up the mountainside." He'd climbed about forty feet and was hiding behind a tree when the men passed him, following the sound of his retreating horse.

Billy was safe, but was sorry to have lost his horse. He hurried on foot for several miles to the next Pony Express station. He reported what had happened and was soon part of a posse of twenty men headed to the thieves' dugout. It was empty. "We found a newly made grave where they had buried the man I had to kill, and a trail leading southwest toward Denver. That was all. But my adventure at least resulted in clearing the country of horse thieves."

Billy returned to work and soon learned that his time as a Pony Express rider was coming to a close. Even though the Pony Express carried an average of seven hundred letters a week—each at the cost of five dollars per half ounce to the sender—its operational expenses were so great that the venture nearly

The Pony Express transmitted news coast-to-coast in days instead of months, helping to unify the country, but the telegraph was even faster.

bankrupted Russell, Majors & Waddell. At the same time, the rapid expansion of telegraph lines from coast-to-coast, which offered cheaper and more reliable communication, delivered the final blow.

The Pony Express lasted for sixteen months during the years 1860 and 1861. It had 80 riders, 500 horses, and 190 stations. While it was in operation it fired the public's imagination and gave its riders the experience of a lifetime. To this day it comprises one of the most dramatic chapters in the history of transportation. Billy could never have dreamed that one day the most famous name associated with it would be his own.

CHAPTER 17

BILLY'S VOLUNTEER WAR

◆·◆

Billy was fifteen when the Pony Express ended in the fall of 1861. He returned home to the Salt Creek Valley and found it in an uproar: the Civil War had officially begun.

Apart from the war itself, the year 1861 was momentous for Kansas. It had taken the election of Abraham Lincoln in November 1860 and then the secession of several Southern states to make statehood for Kansas a reality. Only then, after several proposed state constitutions from both pro- and anti-slave factions were rejected, could anti-slave members of Congress push through the approval of a constitution submitted by the Kansas Free State Party.

Kansas had endured seven years of violence and bloodshed, six governors, and two opposing legislatures before it entered the Union as a free state on January 29, 1861, claiming the thirty-fourth star on

$200 Reward!

Ranaway from the sub-scriber, living in Saline county, on the 4th inst., two Negro men, named Jim and Jack---each aged about 25 years.

Jim

is dish-faced; has sore eyes and bad teeth; is of a light black or brown color; speaks quick, is about 5 feet 7 inches high; had on when last seen, blue cotton pants, white shirt, white fulled coat and new custom-made boots.

Jack

had on the same kind of clothing with shoes, has a very small foot, wears perhaps a No. 6 shoe, and has heavy tacks in the heels; is about the same height and color of Jim. They are doubtless aiming for K. T. **A reward of $100 each will be** given if taken outside of the State, or $50 each if taken in the State, outside of Saline county. **G. D. WILLIAMS,**

Spring Garden, P. O., Pettis county, Missouri.
Harrisonville, Mo., June 7th, 1860.

Slaves escaping to freedom in Kansas were an ongoing problem for Missouri slaveholders. This reward poster notes, "They are doubtless aiming for K.T." (Kansas Territory).

the American flag and fighting with the Union during the Civil War. But next door in Missouri, everything was a toss-up. It was a slave state, yet many Missourians opposed slavery. Of those who supported slavery, many were still loyal to the Union. Confederate sympathizers set up their own government at Neosho, Missouri, and it was officially recognized by the Confederacy. Thereafter, though technically part of the Union, Missouri had two governments. Jefferson City sent 110,000 recruits to the Union army, while Neosho sent 40,000 to the Confederate army. Missouri had its star on both the Union and Confederate flags. All this divisiveness kept the state in turmoil.

Back in Kansas, statehood was bittersweet in the Cody household. Billy's father had helped make Kansas a free state and had given his life for the cause. His sacrifice would forever be a terrible burden for his family. "I miss Mr. Cody so much," Mary Cody wrote to a friend. She spoke of how ill she was and of her mounting financial problems. At the end of the letter she declared how much she loved her children, noting of Billy that he "is one of the smartest and best of boys, he has always been a great comfort to me."

Though Mary Cody was a strong Unionist, she was fearful that if Billy became a soldier he would be killed. At age fifteen he was officially too young to enlist—but at least a quarter of the soldiers who fought in the Civil War were under the legal age of eighteen. "Many of my boyhood friends were enlisting," Billy said. "I was eager to join them. But I was still the breadwinner of the family. Not because of this, but because of her love for me, my mother exacted from me a promise that I would not enlist for the war while she lived."

So Billy stayed home the summer of 1861, working whatever jobs he could get. Everywhere he went, he heard talk about war. The first major battle west of the Mississippi River was fought at

Wilson's Creek, near Springfield, Missouri, on August 10. The Confederate victory gave the South a real boost.

Discord along the Kansas-Missouri border had slowed while Billy was out West, but it burst into flames when the Civil War officially started. This time, Kansans were as violent as Missourians. Jim Lane of Lawrence led a vengeful band of Kansas guerillas. His old rival, Charles Robinson, now the governor of Kansas, feared that Lane would incite Missourians to bloody retaliation and stated, "If our towns and settlements are laid waste by fire and sword . . . we will have General Lane to thank for it."

Guerrilla fighters from Kansas became known as Jayhawkers, named for the Jayhawk—a mythical bird described by admirers as brave and bold, though to Missourians, Jayhawkers were murderers and thieves. Missouri border ruffians were now called Bushwhackers, supposedly because they stayed out in the bush, away from towns and law enforcement.

Although these bands of guerrilla irregulars could be helpful to the Union or Confederate armies, neither the law nor the military could control them. Tracking them down was almost impossible, for they wore no uniforms and were supported and sheltered by local people.

Both sides committed atrocities. One of the worst occurred just a month after the Union loss at Wilson's Creek, when Jim Lane and his Jayhawkers descended on Osceola, a Missouri town of 2,500 people on the banks of the Osage River. They pillaged stores, homes, barns, and churches, and executed nine citizens in the public square. They also rounded up hundreds of horses and mules along with all the loot they could carry. Before they left they set the city ablaze. "As the sun went down . . . Osceola was a heap of smoldering ruins," said an eyewitness. Lane's troops marched back to Kansas followed by hundreds of slaves eager to gain their freedom.

Missourians vowed revenge for Osceola—and they would get it.

Mary Cody warned Billy not to get involved in raids into Missouri. Lawlessness was not the answer, she argued. But the family had suffered greatly, and Billy wanted to even the score. In Leavenworth he found companions who, "like our family, [had] lost everything at the hands of the Missourians," Billy said. He joined with twenty-five others "for the purpose of invading Missouri and making war on its people." He did not tell his mother.

Billy reasoned that he and the others weren't Jayhawkers—they weren't going to burn homes or kill anybody, they were only going to steal some horses. He justified his actions by reasoning that Missouri was a slave state and "the inhabitants must all be secessionists, and therefore our enemies."

On the designated night, the gang met near Westport, Missouri, just across the border from Kansas. Stealing horses was child's play for Billy. He and the others returned with several horses each. Billy sold his and gave his mother the money without telling her the source.

"This action may look . . . like horse-stealing, and some people might not hesitate to call it by that name," Billy said. "But [we] plausibly maintained that we were only getting back our own, or the equivalent, from the Missourians, and as the government was waging war against the South, it was perfectly square and honest, and we had a good right to do it. So we didn't let our consciences trouble us very much."

Soon Billy rode regularly with the gang. "We continued to make similar raids on the Missourians off and on during the summer, and occasionally we had running fights with them; none of the skirmishes, however, amounting to much."

When Kansas lawmen came after the gang, several of Billy's cohorts were arrested for horse stealing. Somehow Mary Cody found out that Billy was involved. "My mother, upon learning that I was engaged in this business, told me I was neither honorable nor right, and she would not for a moment countenance any such proceedings."

Because of his deep respect for her, that was the end of Billy's foray as a horse thief. He quit, stating, "I abandoned the Jayhawking enterprise, for such it really was."

Jayhawkers inflicted terrible damage on Missourians, stealing horses, plundering personal property, and destroying homes and farms.

CHAPTER 18

BILLY JOINS
THE RED LEGS

◆ ◆ ◆

W hat work sixteen-year-old Billy could find was usually for the army or Russell, Majors & Waddell. Most jobs kept him close to home, but once he carried military dispatches to Fort Larned in central Kansas, and another time he went with several men on a trip to buy horses for the army. He even met up with Wild Bill long enough to serve as his assistant wagon master, delivering government supplies to Springfield and Rolla, Missouri.

In the spring of 1862 he took on a longer assignment, serving as a guide and a scout for an army regiment heading into Kiowa and Comanche territory on the Santa Fe Trail, where the tribes were attacking travelers. Although the country was torn apart by the war, Abraham Lincoln's government had stayed vigilant to the

Custer ordered the Washita massacre, pictured here, killing peaceful Cheyenne on their reservation. Because the American military had superior numbers and weapons, Indian resistance was ultimately doomed.

"Indian problem." Billy was in his element. He liked and respected almost all Native Americans, but he felt that they had to accept the reality of whites moving into their territory and to learn to live peacefully with them. He felt that only the fear of reprisal by the US government would convince them.

When he returned home at the end of the summer, Billy found work carrying military dispatches, and he grudgingly attended school when he had the time. He was full-grown now—just over six feet tall, strongly built, with posture straight as an arrow. From the age of eight he had taken on jobs that were challenging even for adults and had done them well. This had filled him with self-confidence. Men admired him: he was a skillful hunter and tracker, scout and guide. And as Billy was starting to realize, women found him charming, courteous, chivalrous—and very handsome. He turned heads wherever he went.

Though he kept his promise to his mother not to join the army, Bushwhackers were threatening the area, and it needed to be defended. Billy had turned seventeen when he became a Jayhawker once again. This time he was open about it with his mother. "I felt I could join without breaking my promise not to enlist for the war, and join it I did," he said.

He rode with one of the most infamous Jayhawker bands of them all, the Red Legs. The name came from the red stockings its members wore while on a mission. The leader of Billy's group was a cold, hard man, Captain Bill Tuff, who had a reputation for cruelty; he had been known to hang captured Bushwhackers. "We had plenty to do," Billy reported. "The [Missouri] guerrillas were daring fellows and kept us busy. They robbed banks, raided villages, burned buildings, and looted and plundered."

But the Red Legs did the same. When they crossed into Missouri, they didn't care which side their victims supported. "The Red Legs are desolating the country, they have no respect for any person's political opinions," one Missourian said. A historian noted that "a full recital of their deeds would sound like the biography of devils."

Both Kansans and Missourians were forming home guards or militias to try to protect themselves and their property from Bushwhackers and Jayhawkers. Billy's family thought he was involved only in protecting Kansans and their property. Julia naively commented that "the Red-Leggers were proud that despite numerous provocations they did not copy the enemy's tactics but restricted themselves to purely defensive fighting."

It's doubtful that Billy set her straight. "We were the biggest gang of thieves on record," he later admitted. He said little of his participation, merely commenting that "we had many a lively skirmish with the Bushwhackers . . . and when we were not hunting them . . . we had a very festive time. We . . . ran things to suit ourselves."

When the Red Legs "ran things," it was usually at the expense of others.

The Kansas-Missouri border was under the jurisdiction of the US government, and the Union general Thomas Ewing was in charge of border security. As part of his strategy against the Bushwhackers, Ewing rounded up some of their relatives. His plan was to force these family members to leave the area, believing that the Bushwhackers would then follow them. Union troops temporarily locked up a dozen girls and young women—most of them the sisters or sweethearts of Bushwhackers—in a decrepit building in Kansas City. Tragically, the building collapsed, killing five of the girls and severely injuring several others.

This incident filled Bushwhackers with rage. It called for a special kind of revenge. That summer of 1863, a leader emerged who would see that they got it. His name was William Clarke Quantrill.

OPPOSITE: Celebrating on the frontier usually meant drinking, gambling, and getting rowdy. Some towns required men entering saloons to hang up their guns or turn them over to the sheriff.

CHAPTER 19

QUANTRILL TAKES REVENGE

◆•◆

Billy knew who Quantrill was. As one of the Red Legs, Billy was committed to protecting Kansas against Quantrill and others like him. But he wasn't able to help Kansans defend themselves against Quantrill when they needed it the most. Billy was working on a wagon train headed to Colorado when Quantrill masterminded the biggest and bloodiest event to occur in Kansas during the war: the Lawrence massacre known as Quantrill's Raid.

Quantrill, a brutal Bushwhacker with a loyal band of followers, wanted revenge for all the atrocities perpetrated on Missourians by groups like Billy's Red Legs. The prosperous abolitionist stronghold of Lawrence had already been a pro-slave target several times, and now it became Quantrill's target as well.

His guerillas were mostly teenagers like Billy. Some were as young as fifteen. The most feared was "Bloody Bill" Anderson, whose sister had died in the Kansas City building collapse. Two other sisters had been seriously injured. For Bloody Bill, it was payback time. "Lawrence or hell," he declared, "but with one proviso, that we kill every male thing."

Cole Younger, who would become an outlaw after the war, was also with Quantrill, for he, too, had family who had suffered at the hands of Kansans. So did the future outlaw Frank James, the brother of Jesse James, who joined Quantrill in the spring of 1863. "We all loved him," James said of their leader. "He was a demon in battle and did not know how to be afraid."

Tall and lean, stylishly dressed, with fair hair and a finely groomed moustache, twenty-six-year-old Quantrill carried six loaded pistols: two in holsters and four stuck in his belt. He'd grown up in Ohio and moved to Kansas in 1857. He farmed, taught school, and lived briefly in Lawrence before joining the Bushwhackers.

Because of his time in Lawrence, he knew which families were

Although Quantrill is shown in this drawing in a Confederate uniform, sources differ as to whether he was ever officially commissioned into the Confederate service.

wealthy, where the banks were, and what businesses were worth robbing. He knew that the city's warehouses were stocked with goods and its stables full of prime horses. The only military forces in the area were twenty African-American soldiers on leave from Fort Leavenworth, twenty-two young army recruits, and a dozen soldiers stationed on the other side of the river. Many able-bodied Lawrence males were away, serving in militia groups or in the army.

There were other reasons why Quantrill's target was Lawrence. The town served as the headquarters for the Red Legs, and goods that the Red Legs stole from their Missouri victims were openly auctioned there. Another reason was that many inhabitants of Lawrence were active in the Underground Railroad, providing shelter for slaves who had escaped their Missouri masters. Finally, Isaac Cody's friends, including the abolitionist Charles Robinson, who until a few months earlier had been governor of Kansas, lived in Lawrence, and so did the Jayhawker Jim Lane, who had plundered and burned Osceola. Lane was at the top of the death list that Quantrill carried with him.

A rumor had circulated in Lawrence several weeks earlier that Quantrill might try a raid, for he and his men had recently plundered and burned the nearby settlements of Olathe and Shawnee. The rumor had caused a great flurry, but nothing had come of it, and the community was lulled back into a false sense of security.

Lawrence was fifty miles from the Missouri border. If there was a threat, the citizens of the town thought they'd find out in plenty of time to defend themselves.

Indeed, several people tried to sound the alarm after spotting Quantrill's men on the march, but none made it to Lawrence in time. Others saw the men and assumed they were Union troops, for Quantrill had them ride in army formation. Some even wore regimental blue shirts to make them look like Yankee soldiers An observer seeing them up close would have noticed that many of them

---

Quantrill and his men moved quietly through the early dawn light on their murderous mission to attack Lawrence.

had long hair—the style favored by the Bushwhackers—but anyone coming that close to the men would have been shot.

August 21, 1863, dawned as a hot, sultry day. Much of Lawrence was asleep at 5:00 a.m. when Quantrill's scouts reported that no lookouts were posted in the town. Quantrill addressed the 450 Bushwhackers with him, telling them that women and children were not to be harmed, but that adult males, and any boys old enough to take up arms, were to be killed on sight. Those wearing blue shirts shed them. Then, on signal, they thundered into town, guns blazing, with cries of "Remember Osceola!" or the names of the girls killed in the jail's collapse.

Charles Robinson was on his way to his barn for an early morning ride when he saw the raiders entering Lawrence. He realized immediately what was happening and hastily hid. He knew that if there was a death list, he was on it.

Chaos erupted as the Bushwhackers roared through the streets. Horsemen were suddenly everywhere. Gunfire and smoke filled the air. Everyone seemed to be running, but no one knew what to do or where to go. Among the first victims were the young army recruits asleep in their tents. Seventeen of the twenty-two were killed. The Bushwhackers cordoned off the downtown area and stormed along Massachusetts Street, shooting every man and teenage boy they encountered.

Several Bushwhackers headed straight to the river to cut the

Newspapers in the North portrayed Quantrill's Raid as "wanton brutality" and "cold-blooded murder." In contrast, Southern newspapers said Quantrill was a hero.

ferry cable and prevent escape by boat. The dozen Union troops on other side of the river saw the American flag being taken down and trampled on. They started to shoot across the water, but they were too far away to hit anything.

Quantrill and his men entered every business, looting and destroying everything in their path. Two banks were robbed, and the offices of the town's three anti-slave newspapers were ransacked and burned. The school, the county courthouse, and several churches were destroyed. Townspeople were stripped of pocket watches, jewelry, and money. At the Free State Hotel, which had been rebuilt in even grander style after being destroyed in the 1856 raid, Bushwhackers burst into rooms and robbed frightened guests, then set the hotel on fire. Many of the Bushwhackers got drunk on liquor stolen from homes or demanded at gunpoint in downtown saloons.

The raiders fanned out across town, barging into homes or shooting their way in. Men were dragged outside and shot point-blank, often in front of their families. Once the Bushwhackers had stolen everything they could, they set the homes on fire. Some forbade women to save even a precious photo or their marriage license, while others actually helped women move their possessions outside before burning their houses.

Men tried to hide in fields, ravines, barns, and wells. Many of those who hid in cellars and attics were discovered and shot or burned out. A few men survived by begging for their lives or saying they were Southern sympathizers. Several revealed later that they had disguised themselves as women, just as Isaac Cody had once done when pro-slavers came to the Codys' farm to try to kill him. One woman rolled up her husband in a carpet that she dragged outside her home along with the other household belongings she was trying to save.

Quantrill's men stood by as she wrestled with the heavy carpet, and then they torched the house. But her husband was saved.

Jim Lane lived in a lavish brick home opulently furnished with plunder stolen from Missourians during his many raids. When he heard the commotion in the streets, he fled out the back door and into a field, still wearing his nightshirt. Quantrill's greatest disappointment that day was that he didn't capture Lane, for he had planned to take him back to Missouri and hang him.

As Billy would later learn, most of what happened that early August morning in 1863 was grim. The killings ended at 9:00 a.m., when Quantrill received word that federal troops were coming. By then, much of Lawrence was on fire, and billowing smoke could be seen for miles away. Quantrill rounded up his men, many of them very drunk. They rode out of town carrying and dragging all the loot they could. Large items like pianos were loaded into wagons, with stolen horses tethered to the back.

They left behind a devastated community of three thousand citizens. One hundred and fifty boys and men had been murdered, including all twenty of the African-American soldiers on leave from Fort Leavenworth. The victims were carried to the Methodist church and laid out on the floor. Funerals began almost immediately. As Quantrill had ordered, no women or young children had been injured, but their lives would never again be the same. Lawrence was now a community of fatherless children and widows.

Sara Robinson was not one of them. As smoke billowed into the August sky, Charles Robinson emerged from hiding and was tearfully reunited with his wife, who until that moment had thought him dead.

When Quantrill and his men rode out of Lawrence, they left behind a burning city.

CHAPTER 20

MOTHER

◆–•–◆

When Billy's wagon train reached the Denver area in September 1863, he was shocked to learn about Quantrill's raid on Lawrence, but even more distressed when he found a letter waiting for him. Julia's words were urgent: their mother was dying.

He hastened home, arriving in time to receive his mother's blessing and to say a last good-bye. Billy would always think of his mother as noble, brave, and loyal. "I loved her above all other persons," he said. Almost fifty years later, in 1910, he wrote in a letter to a friend, "I grew up among some of the roughest men and some of the most desperate characters that ever infested the border of civilization. And had it not been for [the] teaching and prayers of my mother, I might have died with my boots on."

The family buried Mary Cody next to Isaac in the Leavenworth cemetery. Then they took a hard look at the future. Billy did not have to worry about the care of his four sisters and little brother, for the previous year Julia had married a neighboring farmer, an older man who was willing to serve as a guardian to the younger children. With Billy's financial help, the family could all continue to live in their Salt Creek Valley home.

Grief for his mother left Billy barely able to function. He went to stay in Leavenworth, where for two months he led what he later called "a dissolute and reckless life," associating with "gamblers, drunkards, and bad characters generally."

Billy always credited his mother for her pioneer spirit and her bravery in overcoming every adversity. This 1860 photo is the only one known of her.

He had promised his mother that he would not enlist while she was alive. Perhaps it was no surprise when, he said, "one day, after having been under the influence of bad whiskey, I awoke to find myself a soldier in the Seventh Kansas. I did not remember how or when I had enlisted, but I saw I was in for it, and that it would not do for me to endeavor to back out."

Billy was now a private in the Union army. His sister Helen recalled the family's surprise when Billy showed up in his uniform. "Overwhelmed with grief over Mother's death, it seemed more than we could bear to see our big brother ride off to war. We threatened to inform the recruiting officers that he was not yet eighteen; but he was too thoroughly in earnest to be moved by our objections. The regiment in which he had enlisted was already ordered to the front, and he had come home to say goodbye."

CHAPTER 21

PRIVATE CODY: SCOUT AND SPY

◆ ◆ ◆

Billy entered the army in February 1864, a week before his eighteenth birthday. Among the Seventh Kansas Cavalry, he said, "I found many of my old friends and schoolmates." During his first few months in the service, he participated in skirmishes against Confederate guerillas. In the spring, his unit traveled by steamboat to Memphis to join the fight against Nathan Bedford Forrest. According to Billy, this Confederate general "was making a great deal of trouble in southern Tennessee." No Union general had yet been able to defeat him.

OPPOSITE: As good a scout as Billy was, he also put to work his natural charm, flair for drama, and skill as a storyteller when he served as a spy in the Civil War.

Forrest stood out for his brilliance, his bravery, and his cruelty. Union general William T. Sherman referred to him as a devil, and the entire Union army feared him, for he had been known to massacre soldiers he'd taken as prisoner. To fight Forrest, the Union army first had to find him. Upon learning of Billy's work as a scout, officers recommended him to the commanding general, Andrew Jackson Smith.

Nathan Bedford Forrest was so skillful in battle that General William Sherman declared that there could be no Union victory while he was alive.

General Smith invited Billy into his tent and questioned him closely about his experience as a scout out West. Billy later recalled the meeting: "'You ought to be able to render me valuable service,' Smith said. When I replied that I should be only too glad to do so, he got out a map of Tennessee and on it showed me where he believed General Forrest's command to be located."

Billy's mission was to discover Forrest's exact whereabouts, then go behind enemy lines to learn how many soldiers Forrest had and what his plan of attack was. Smith told Billy that he would need to return as quickly as possible and that

Billy joined a regiment formed by "Doc" Jennison, a Jayhawker and now a Union army colonel who wanted to recruit men who had also been Jayhawkers.

---

the mission was extremely dangerous.

"'If you are captured,' he said, 'you will be shot as a spy.'"

Billy traded his uniform for overalls and a shirt that made him look like a Tennessee farm boy. His horse had the army's brand on it, so he was given his pick of several Tennessee horses. An officer escorted him a mile out of camp and then Billy rode on alone. He made sure to sit on his horse with the easy manner of a country boy instead of that of a disciplined soldier, and he practiced talking in a Southern drawl—an easy task since he had a ready ear for dialects. His horse proved to be excellent and made good time.

The next morning Billy saw a big plantation. "I was anxious to learn how my disguise was going to work, and therefore rode boldly

INDEPENDENT
KANSAS
Jay-Hawkers.

Volunteers are wanted for the 1st Regiment of Kansas Volunteer Cavalry to serve our country

During the War.

Horses will be furnished by the Government. Good horses will be purchased of the owner who volunteers. Each man will be mounted, and armed with a Sharp's Rifle, a Navy Revolver, and a Sabre. The pay will be that of the regular volunteer.

Volunteers from Northern Kansas will rendezvous at Leavenworth. Those from Southern Kansas will rendezvous at Mound City. Volunteers singly, parts of companies and full companies will be mustered into the United States service as soon as they report themselves to the local recruiting officer at either of the above places. Upon arriving at Mound City volunteers will report themselves to John T. Snoddy, Acting Adjutant. Those who rendezvous at Leavenworth will report themselves to D. R. Anthony, Esq. of that place.

C. R. JENNISON,
Col. 1st Regiment Kansas Vol. Cavalry.
MOUND CITY, Aug. 24, 1861.

up to the house and asked if I could rest and get some sort of break-fast. . . . I used my best imitation of the Southern dialect . . . and it was perfectly successful. I was given breakfast, my mare was fed, and I slept most of the day in a haystack, taking up my journey again immediately after dinner."

Now fully confident of his disguise, Billy chatted with anybody he met on the road. Within two days he'd found Forrest's army. Pretending to be a naive country boy, he approached the guards. He told them he had come to see his father and brother, who were fighting with Forrest. The guards let him pass.

Billy got permission to pasture his horse with the Confederates' horses. Then he walked into the camp and began casual conversa-tions with both soldiers and officers. "By acting the part of a rural boy and staring open-mouthed at all the camp life, I picked up a great deal of information without once falling under suspicion." He found out everything he needed to know and then talked his way back through the guards and headed north.

He retraced his route, but this time, because he was traveling toward the Union army, he was careful not to arouse the suspicion of Southerners. "I now made all speed northward, keeping out of sight of houses and strangers. On the second day I passed several detachments of Forrest's troops, but my training as a scout en-abled me to keep them from seeing me. Though my mare had proven herself an animal of splendid endurance, I had to stop and rest her occasionally. At such times I kept closely hidden.

"On the second morning after leaving Forrest's command, I sighted the advance guard of Smith's army. They halted me when I rode up and for a time I had more trouble with them than I'd had with any of Forrest's men."

Billy was taken into custody. He insisted that he was a Union soldier and demanded to see General Smith. Finally the guards gave in. Even Smith failed to recognize him. However, once Billy identified himself, the general greeted him warmly. "My commander was much pleased with my report," Billy said, "which proved to be accurate and valuable."

Smith told him to stay in disguise, that there would be work for him the next day. Billy returned to his own men, who peppered him with questions about where he'd been. But Billy knew that spies could be anywhere and refused to tell them anything.

The next morning when he rode out with the entire command to pursue Forrest's army, everyone seemed to know he'd been on a scouting trip, for wherever he went, he was cheered by the men. Smith soon sent him on ahead of the troops, telling him, "if you see anything that I ought to know about, come back and tell me."

Still dressed in his disguise and happy to be a scout once again, Billy started out. Soon he came upon an elegant home that sat close to the road. A woman and her two teenage daughters watched him from the porch. Billy thought immediately of his mother and sisters and the dangers they had faced when Bushwhackers and border ruffians had threatened everyone in the Salt Creek Valley. His protective instincts urged him forward. "They were greatly alarmed when I came up, and asked if I didn't know that the Yankee army would be along in a few minutes and that my life was in peril. All their own men folks, they said, were hiding in the timber."

Billy asked for a glass of milk. They got it for him. "But you must leave quickly!" they urged. Instead he stayed on the porch in full view of the road. The mother was frantic. "Don't you sit here! The Yankee troops will go right through this house. They will break up the piano and every stick of furniture, and leave the place in ruins. You are sure to be killed or taken prisoner."

Billy remained where he was. "I resolved to do what I could to protect them," he said. "By this time the advance guard was coming up the road. General Smith passed . . . I saw that he had noticed me, though he gave no sign of having done so. As more troops passed, men began leaving their companies and rushing toward the house. I ordered them away in the name of the General. They all knew who I was and obeyed, much to the astonishment of the lady and her daughters. Turning to my hostess, I said, 'Madam, I can't keep them out of your chicken house or your smokehouse or your storerooms, but I can keep them out of your home, and I will.' I remained on the porch till the entire command had passed. Nothing was molested."

The women had already figured out that Billy was a Yankee. As grateful as they were that he had saved their home, they feared that their men would kill him when they returned from the woods. Just then the men burst through the back door. The mother "leaped between them and me," Billy recalled. "'Don't shoot him!' she cried. 'He has protected our property and our lives!'" But the men merely wanted to add their thanks, for they had been watching and knew what Billy had done.

As the adults laid out their best food for their guest, the daughters flirted with Billy. "I was most agreeably entertained by the young ladies," he said. They filled his haversack with food and a bottle of fine peach brandy while Billy talked about his mother, his little brother, and his sisters. He confirmed that he was a Union scout, and that he would have to answer for what he'd done, since the orders were to destroy all Southern property. He hoped the brandy would soften General Smith's reaction when he found out.

Billy said his good-byes and was soon back with the troops, satisfied that he had helped a Confederate family save its home. He quickly found General Smith, who took the brandy gratefully but questioned Billy about disobeying orders. "A lady and her two daughters were alone there," he replied. "My mother had suffered from raids of hostile soldiers in Kansas. I tried to protect [this woman], as I would have liked another man to protect my mother in her distress."

General Smith considered this for a moment. "'My boy,' he said, 'you may be too good-hearted for a soldier, but you have done just what I would have done. . . . We will forget your violation.'"

CHAPTER 22

A SOLDIER'S LIFE

◆•◆

Billy loved to talk about his adventures during the Civil War, but he rarely ever spoke of his experiences on the battlefield. He saw it all—the carnage and suffering, the acts of bravery and of cowardice—for he participated in many battles. He did not complain about marching through mud, rain, freezing cold, and blazing heat, or the bad food, filth, and hardship of camp life. He did not criticize or ridicule his leaders. He was a good soldier. In helping a Southern family keep its home a little longer, he retained his humanity in the midst of war.

Those who knew him during the war confirmed that he was an excellent soldier. But he was also a frontiersman, and whenever he was in battle, his first instinct was to find cover. Civil War soldiers were taught to kneel in place and fire, even when totally in the open. This made no sense to Billy, whose first instinct was always to find cover if it was available. He was not surprised when other soldiers copied him.

Billy and his regiment were in the thick of the fighting at Tupelo, Mississippi, on July 14, 1864, when General Smith defeated Nathan Bedford Forrest. Billy's regiment went on to fight at Hurricane Creek

---

Billy is not in this 1862 photo, but it shows enlisted men in the Eighth Kansas Infantry.

and at Oxford, Mississippi. Then they boarded steamboats headed north on the Mississippi River, for they were needed in Missouri. General Sterling Price, the Confederate leader who had won the Missouri battles of Lexington and Wilson's Creek early in the war, had amassed a large army and was bent on claiming both Missouri and Kansas for the Confederacy.

For the next six weeks, Billy's regiment saw daily action against Price. Some of that time Billy worked as a messenger and a spy, carrying dispatches from Union general to Union general. He often passed through Confederate lines disguised as a Confederate soldier. He was never caught. On one spy mission to learn what he could about Price's movements, he rode up to a farmhouse dressed in Confederate gray, hoping for a meal. The farmwife showed him into the kitchen, where a man dressed as a Confederate officer was eating alone at the table.

Billy's jaw dropped. There sat his old friend Wild Bill Hickok! Wild Bill just grinned at him. "You little rascal," he said. The two men shared bread and milk—the only food the farmwife had to offer—while catching up on news. Wild Bill paid for their meal, and the two went outside where they could talk in private.

Like Billy, Wild Bill was working as a Union spy and had successfully infiltrated Price's Confederate lines. He shared with Billy what he knew. Billy thanked him and then told Wild Bill about his mother's recent death. "He was greatly surprised and grieved," Billy said, "for she had treated him almost as one of her own children." The two men warmly shook hands and then parted, not knowing when—or if—they might ever see each other again.

After Billy and his fellow soldiers helped prevent Price's capture of Saint Louis, Price turned his troops toward pro-Union Kansas City, which straddled the Kansas-Missouri border and had four thousand residents. Price's goal was to occupy Kansas City and then move westward to attack Fort Leavenworth—his first step in conquering Kansas. Billy's regiment and other Union troops confronted Price twice east of Kansas City, and both times Price defeated them.

But Price ran out of luck. He was badly outnumbered when he reached the Kansas City area and was eventually defeated in the bloody three-day Battle of Westport, which began on October 23, 1864, and involved 23,000 Confederate and Union soldiers. Though Billy escaped injury, his regiment was in the middle of the action and suffered many casualties. The Battle of Westport became known as the Gettysburg of the West, for Price's loss there ensured that Missouri was finally and forever a Union state.

Price and his army fled southward through Kansas. Union troops, including Billy, pursued them, repeatedly engaging them in battle. Bushwhackers were traveling with Price, and all along the way they attacked settlers, burning and killing as part of their last painful thrust at Kansas. Hundreds of wagons were filled with stolen loot, everything from bedding and furniture to farm tools

A Kansas soldier created this painting showing Confederate soldiers guarding Union infantry taken prisoner during the Battle of Westport.

and saddles, and most of it was discarded along the way. When Price lost a furious battle at Mine Creek, he hastily retreated, leaving his dead, wounded, and exhausted men behind. Union forces pursued him to the Arkansas border and then turned back. Price's army had disintegrated. Everyone knew that the Confederates would never again be a threat to Kansas or Missouri.

Billy fought long and hard throughout the campaign to defeat

Price. Later he enjoyed telling the story of how he was with a scouting party that surprised several of Price's officers near Mound City, Kansas, forcing them to surrender. "While we were rounding them up I heard one of them say that we Yanks had captured a bigger prize than we suspected. 'That big man over yonder is General Marmaduke of the Southern Army,'" they said.

John Marmaduke was a Missouri native and a well-known Confederate army general. Billy was impressed: "I had heard much of Marmaduke and greatly admired his dash and ability as a fighting man." Billing introduced himself and asked the general if he needed anything. When Marmaduke mentioned that he was hungry, Billy shared what food he had in his saddlebag. Later he was assigned to take Marmaduke to prison at Fort Leavenworth. Although they fought on opposite sides, Billy said, "The General and I became fast friends, and our friendship lasted long after the war."

This was the kind of war story he liked to tell.

The Civil War officially ended in April 1865. The following September, Billy was mustered out as a private. He had served nearly twenty months and was nineteen years old. He wanted to go home and be with his sisters, for once again they were grieving a death in the family. Their little brother, Charlie, had died during an epidemic of typhoid fever in 1864 at the age of nine.

Bleeding Kansas and the Civil War were in the past. Billy's focus was on the future.

CHAPTER 23

BECOMING BUFFALO BILL

◆·◆·◆

As Kansas began its recovery from eleven years of war and turmoil, Billy barreled into adulthood. He was stationed briefly in Saint Louis during his final months in the army, and there he met the beautiful, dark-eyed Louisa Frederici. He parted with her long enough to serve as a guide for William Tecumseh Sherman, the famous Civil War general, on a trip through the West.

In March of 1866, Billy returned to Saint Louis and married Louisa. He was barely twenty and she was twenty-two. She wanted him to be a businessman and Billy agreed to try, provided they moved to Leavenworth so he could be close to his sisters. There he was hired to manage a small hotel, but he still longed to go west, an option Louisa wouldn't discuss.

When the hotel failed, he needed a way to support a family, for Louisa was pregnant. She reluctantly agreed to stay with her parents in Saint Louis while Billy headed west—but not too far west—in search of work. Because of his experience guiding Sherman, he was quickly hired by the army as a scout and guide. This was what he loved to do, but his paycheck was small, and he never had quite enough income to support both Louisa and his sisters.

The army was using force to try to subdue native tribes unwilling to voluntarily move onto reservations. In defiance, these tribes were attacking both settlers and soldiers. One of Billy's first assignments was guiding General George Armstrong Custer against them. He also helped a detachment of buffalo soldiers—almost all of them freed slaves—escape an Indian massacre.

He was thrilled with the birth of his daughter, Arta, and he tried

Arta Cody was nine in this photo with her parents.

again to settle down, taking a job as a buffalo hunter with the railroad in central Kansas to supply meat for the workers building the tracks. Louisa lived close by with the baby.

With an estimated twelve million buffalo roaming the plains, no one thought they would ever become extinct. Billy did his job well and killed thousands. He was so skillful a shot that he could usually down a buffalo with one bullet. Amazed by his prowess, the railroad workers dubbed him "Buffalo Bill," and the name stuck. From then on he was called either Buffalo Bill or just Bill, but he was no longer Billy.

It's thought that the railroad workers made up this jingle about him:

> *Buffalo Bill, Buffalo Bill,*
> *Never missed and never will;*
> *Always aims and shoots to kill*
> *And the company pays his buffalo bill.*

When his railroad job ended, Bill went back to work for the army, beginning a fifteen-year period of working either with the army or as a scout and a guide in western Nebraska. During that time he began the journey that led to his Wild West show. One day in 1869 he met a writer named Ned Buntline who was looking for

With the assistance of a well-trained horse, Billy could drive a buffalo close to camp before shooting it. That way, the carcass didn't have to be retrieved from the prairie.

ideas for his dime novels—cheap, sensational "blood and thunder" fiction aimed at a mass readership. Bill loved to spin yarns and tell stories—a skill he'd learned sitting around all those camp-fires with frontiersmen and soldiers—so he regaled Buntline with some of them. The next thing he knew, Buntline had published a dime novel titled *Buffalo Bill, the King of Border Men*. Bill was flattered, but since the book was fiction he gave it little thought. Nor was he paid anything for it.

The following year, 1870, Louisa gave birth to their son. A proud Bill named him Kit Carson Cody in honor of the legendary scout he so admired. With a growing family to support, he took on extra guide jobs. Duke Alexis of Russia, the third son of Czar Alexander, was touring America and wanted to participate in a buffalo hunt. He hired Bill as his guide, and Bill worked hard to make an impression with his riding and hunting skills, hoping it would lead to more work

Bill carefully created the persona of Buffalo Bill. His hat, long hair, fringed jacket, and high boots were all part of his image. He is twenty-four in this photo.

guiding wealthy people on hunts. He knew that image was important—he'd learned that lesson well from all the colorful mountain men, Indians, and soldiers he'd known. So to add to his own image, he wore fringed buckskin and rode a snow-white horse. Being known as Buffalo Bill helped, too.

Newspaper reporters from the East who were covering the duke's adventures loved everything about this handsome Westerner and mentioned him in their articles. Soon, just as he'd hoped, he was booking work with wealthy Easterners who were eager to experience the West and shoot buffalo. At the same time, Ned Buntline wrote more dime novels about the fictitious exploits of Buffalo Bill. The real Buffalo Bill was becoming famous and wasn't even aware of it.

In 1872, when Bill was twenty-six, he was invited to visit New York City as the guest of several wealthy businessmen he had guided on a hunt. Louisa gave her consent, and he boarded a train for the East. He refused to cut his hair, and he did not own a suit, so he wore his buckskin, at least until one of his sponsors bought him a suit. He left behind the brace of pistols he normally wore, but he took a long fur overcoat that the Russian duke had given him.

In New York he became the toast of the city, for New Yorkers had read about him in the newspaper and knew the dime novels supposedly based on him. They loved this frontiersman with his flowing hair and funny stories, and they entertained him in grand style at parties and dinners. Ned Buntline was in the city staging a play about his Buffalo Bill character, and he urged Bill to attend the opening night. When it was announced that the real Buffalo Bill was there, the audience went wild and Bill was coaxed to the stage. He'd never been on a stage before and was too overcome with stage fright to say a word. Even so, that experience made him realize that people were willing to pay to see a genuine man of the Old West.

He was still flat broke when he returned to Nebraska—unlike Ned Buntline, who was making money from his fictional Buffalo Bill.

Surely, Bill thought, he could also make money, since he was the real Buffalo Bill—just as long as he didn't have to speak any lines.

Before he could figure out how to do this, the army needed him back to help fight the Indians. He was often in danger over the next several months. One time he single-handedly defeated a small group of attacking Indian warriors and recovered horses stolen from the army. In recognition of his bravery he was awarded the Congressional Medal of Honor in 1872. Always modest, he made no fuss about the medal. It was his view that others had conducted themselves just as bravely—he'd merely had eyewitnesses who nominated him.

Bill loved working as a guide and scout for the army, but the pay was poor.

His second daughter, Ora Maude, was also born in 1872. Bill and his family lived at Fort McPherson in Nebraska, and Louisa remained unhappy about his long absences and low pay. When the situation with the tribes grew better and the army didn't need Bill's services, he decided that to make money he would risk going on the stage, for Ned Buntline was urging him to come to Chicago and play himself in a theater production.

Bill did his best, but while he loved to tell stories and enjoyed hearing an audience applaud him, he couldn't learn lines and still suffered from stage fright. Buntline resorted to having him *ad lib* his part, which helped. The audience didn't seem to notice any problem. The show was popular enough that Buntline took it on the road to several cities. But when the tour was over, Bill learned that once again, the only one who'd made very much money was Ned Buntline.

The following year Bill cobbled together his own show—a melodrama about frontier scouts fighting Indians. He had other actors perform with him, and he also talked Wild Bill Hickok into joining him on stage. Unfortunately, Wild Bill proved to be a worse actor than Bill. Plus, he refused to do what he was told, either onstage or off. The two men were able to part as friends. After another year onstage, Bill knew he might not be an actor, but he liked being part of something entertaining. He did well in front of crowds as long as he didn't have to memorize and speak lines. And the crowds adored him.

In 1875 and 1876, he spent part of his time onstage, work that paid the bills, and part of his time as a scout for the army, the work he loved. When the Sioux War broke out in 1876, he left the stage and went back to work for the army. Three weeks after the June 25 defeat of Custer at the Battle of the Little Bighorn, Bill distinguished himself by killing a Northern Cheyenne chief named Yellow Hair in a skirmish between the army and the Indians. Because Yellow Hair (sometimes called "Yellow Hand,") had fought against Custer, the army and the public considered Bill a hero.

But Bill was finished with fighting and killing. They had been his life for too long. Show business looked like the best way to support his family, and fake bullets didn't hurt anyone. He had a big idea in mind, and it was time to bring it to life.

CHAPTER 24

BUFFALO BILL'S WILD WEST

Bill wanted to create a show that would introduce audiences to the West he'd known and loved as a boy. The American frontier was quickly fading, and Americans were nostalgic for stories about bygone days of glory in the Old West.

His vision of a show included sharpshooting competitions, races, and skits that told stories about the Pony Express, prairie fires, and stagecoach rides. The buffalo was nearly extinct, so Bill wanted folks to experience the excitement of what a buffalo hunt had been like, too.

He would be a part of everything, of course, playing the heroic

Western man that audiences loved. But most important to his show would be Native Americans—real ones. Almost all the tribes were now confined to reservations, and few Americans knew much about them.

The entertainment extravaganza he dreamed up ultimately became known as Buffalo Bill's Wild West and Congress of Rough Riders of the World. Even though it was a show, Bill wouldn't allow that word to be part of the title, because, he always said, everything he portrayed was authentic. Regardless of the official name, what he created was an immediate success.

He staged his first performance in Omaha, Nebraska, in 1883. Over the next thirty years, as the show grew in popularity and size, Bill had several different business partners and a team of talented managers who ran the day-to-day operations. They took the show all over America, traveling as many as ten thousand miles each year in a special show train and stopping in as many as one hundred towns. At the show's peak, Bill's train had fifty cars carrying seven hundred entertainers, as well as staff, show animals, costumes, tents, food and cooking supplies, and even a generator for lights for the evening performances. The staff and performers were like a family. It was unique for the times, for it was a mix of races and nationalities—men, women, and children traveling and working together.

Bill (middle of second row, seated) promoted his show as "Buffalo Bill's Wild West—America's National Entertainment." It was a microcosm of race and culture.

Months before Bill's train pulled into a town, his advance team would plaster colorful posters and billboards on buildings, fences, and barns. Merchants were given free tickets in exchange for putting posters in their shop windows. With all this publicity, anticipation reached a frenzy. When the train arrived, crowds of adults and children were always there to greet it, cheering loudly the moment they saw Bill.

The first order of business was unloading the train. Then Bill, riding his fine horse, led everyone—all the performers, the cowboy band, and all the animals—to the show grounds. There, townspeople could watch as the huge tent went up and the arena was assembled. They could admire the Deadwood stagecoach that would figure in several skits and could look on as handlers fed all of the show's animals, including hundreds of horses, as well as mules, elk, deer, bears, and a small herd of buffalo. They could also watch as Native Americans put up their tepees and the rest of the cast and crew pitched their sleeping tents.

Hours before showtime, people started lining up at the entrance so they could get the best seats. Once everyone was settled in, the big moment finally arrived. The cowboy band struck up a rousing tune, and the grand procession began. Hundreds of performers on

---

OPPOSITE: Bill understood the importance of advertising. Colorful posters designed by talented artists were plastered all over towns where the show would play.

foot and horseback entered the arena. The crowd waited breathlessly for the star of the show to appear. And then, finally, there was Buffalo Bill!

As soon as he had greeted celebrities and other special guests in the audience, it was time for action. Bill knew that people liked what he called "noisy, rattling, gunpowder entertainment"—and he gave it to them. A typical performance might begin with pony races

BUFFALO BILL'S WILD WEST

"THE MAZE"

HE MOST ANIMATED EQUESTRIAN SPECTACLE EVER SEEN. A GORGEOUS MOVING PICTURE IN WHICH OVER 300 HEROIC HORSEMEN PARTICIPATE

featuring Mexican, American Indian, and cowboy riders, followed by a skit about the Pony Express in which a young rider demonstrated how riders switched horses with lightning speed.

Sharpshooters were a crowd favorite, and none of them was more famous than Annie Oakley. She was only five feet tall, but she was one of the world's best marksmen. She could shoot with her right or left hand—sideways, backward, or straight-on. She would stand on her horse as it circled the ring and shoot at targets as small as playing cards. For her finale, she would pick up and put down six different shotguns as she shattered eleven glass balls with eleven bullets—all within ten seconds.

Cowboys showed off their skills with the lariat. They rode bucking broncos, and then cowgirls raced ponies against each other. Native Americans performed war dances and attacked the Deadwood stagecoach. They acted in skits about Custer's Last Stand and participated in the buffalo hunt, in which Buffalo Bill showed the audience how he got his famous name, by shooting a buffalo. But he did so with blanks, for now there were no buffalo to spare.

The audience was treated to more races and skits and saw Buffalo Bill demonstrate his own fine shooting skills. Then came the Indian attack on the settler's cabin, with Buffalo Bill riding in to save the day. The evening ended three to four hours after it started, as Buffalo Bill waved and bowed to the elated crowd, who would have gladly sat through another four hours.

Mark Twain wrote to Bill, saying, "I have seen your Wild West show two days in succession, and I have enjoyed it thoroughly. It brought vividly back the breezy wild life of the Great Plains and the Rocky Mountains, and stirred me like a war-song. Down to its smallest details, the show is genuine—cowboys, vaqueros, Indians, stage coach, costumes and all."

The Plains Indians in the show were often a source of controversy. Some people felt that Bill exploited them since they were always the bad guys in the skits, forever chasing someone and always being defeated in the end. But others praised Bill for having them wear ceremonial dress and feathered headdresses, giving them a dignified presence. Two hundred or more native men, women, and children were in the show. A few were Pawnee and the rest were Lakota Sioux. Bill highly regarded the Sioux for their skills in battle. Their great chief Sitting Bull, who had helped defeat Custer at the Little Bighorn, joined the show for a brief four months. He did not participate in skits. Instead he paraded grandly around the arena, ignoring the jeers from people in the audience who were angry at his role in Custer's defeat—something Sitting Bull was proud of.

Bill was occasionally criticized for having Sitting Bull in the show, but he said, "The defeat of Custer was not a massacre. The Indians were being pursued by skilled fighters with orders to kill. . . . They had their wives and little ones to protect and they were fighting for their existence."

Bill paid the Native Americans fair wages—far more than they could earn on the reservation. He treated them respectfully and insisted that everyone who worked for him do so, too. He referred to them as the original Americans, and he featured them on many of his show's posters.

In 1887, Bill was ready for a new adventure and took his Wild West show to Europe. The occasion was the Golden Jubilee celebration of Queen Victoria's fifty years on the throne of England. From there the show would travel to several European cities.

The cast and crew sailed from New York City on the SS *Nebraska* and docked in London two weeks later. On board were 209 performers, including ninety Sioux, plus the crew, and 200 horses, eighteen buffalo, an assortment of other animals, tents, costumes, band instruments, the Deadwood stagecoach, and all the other necessary supplies and equipment.

London was ready for them. The well-known actor Henry Irving had seen the show in the States and had told his fellow Brits, "The most interesting episodes of life on the extreme frontier of civilization in America are represented with the most graphic vividness and scrupulous detail."

The Nebraska National Guard had bestowed the honorary title of "Colonel" on its favorite son. Knowing that the British could be class-conscious, Bill decided to be addressed as "Colonel Cody" on this trip (a title that stuck for the rest of his life). But his show was so popular that a title hardly mattered. Huge crowds from every class of society greeted him wherever he went.

Just as in New York, Bill was the toast of London, and each day his hotel room filled with flowers from female admirers. He was swamped with invitations to parties with royalty. He shared high tea with the famed poet and playwright Oscar Wilde, and he dined with the Prince of Wales and also with Lord and Lady Randolph Churchill, whose thirteen-year-old son, Winston, later saw the show.

In all, the Wild West show would tour Europe eight times, introducing fascinated Europeans to the American West. Cowboy hats became all the rage in Paris, where Buffalo Bill was so beloved that posters announcing his upcoming visits merely showed a picture of him imposed against a buffalo with the words *Je Viens*—"I am coming."

During the Wild West show's 1889 visit to Paris (announced by this poster), Bill introduced Parisians to an American treat: popcorn. It was an instant hit with the French.

But it was that first trip to England that was one of Bill's greatest triumphs. Two particular moments stood out, both involving the queen. She was sixty-eight then, and although she had been widowed for many years, she still wore black and rarely went out in public. Her attendance was the highest honor that could be bestowed on any presentation. She was curious about Buffalo Bill's Wild West show and wanted to see it. The second time, she brought along some members of the European royalty who were attending her jubilee. Bill invited four European kings and the Prince of Wales to ride in the Deadwood stagecoach, then drove it himself at breakneck speed around the arena while whooping Indians chased it. Everyone, including the queen, loved it.

The other moment occurred when Bill rode into the arena as usual, dressed in the finest buckskin, his long hair flowing, carrying a large American flag. With him was Sergeant Bates, a cast member who, like Bill, had fought in the Civil War. The two men

Bill knew that the popularity of his show helped strengthen the bond between Great Britain and the United States.

approached the royal box, where the queen was seated. They stopped their horses directly in front of the queen, and Bill handed the flag to Sergeant Bates, who dipped it to the ground in respect.

Then, to everyone's surprise, a remarkable thing happened: the queen stood and bowed.

It was a stunning moment—an honor for the United States and for Buffalo Bill. The press reported this gesture in glowing terms, noting that no British monarch had ever before given deference to the American flag. While it's possible the queen was only being gracious and meant nothing special by it, this incident advanced Bill's reputation as one of the most famous Americans in the world.

But it didn't change him. Throughout his life, Bill remained the same genuine, caring, optimistic person he'd always been. He was both humble and friendly, and he was interested in everyone, whatever his or her station in life.

Annie Oakley, who was with his show for seventeen years and knew him well, said of him, "His heart never left the great West. Whenever the day's work was done, he could always be found sitting alone watching the sinking sun, and at every opportunity he took the trail back to his old home."

A newspaper reporter wrote that when he met Bill Cody, he liked him immediately. "Everything was done to make Cody conceited and unbearable, but he remained the simple, unassuming child of the plains."

Ultimately, that's who he was: the boy from Bleeding Kansas who created a nineteenth-century icon of the Old West called Buffalo Bill. With that name, he became the greatest showman in history. But he never forgot where he came from. On the inside, he was always Billy Cody.

In this 1905 photo, the fifty-nine-year-old Bill is wearing a popular Stetson hat designed especially for him. The Stetson company called it the "Buffalo Bill."

THE LATER LIFE AND LEGACY
OF THE BOY FROM BLEEDING KANSAS

◆ • ◆

BILL CODY IN THE PUBLIC EYE

Buffalo Bill Cody bridged two centuries. As a boy in Bleeding Kansas, he and his family lived a fairly primitive existence, one often threatened by the violence of war. When he died in 1917 at the age of seventy-one, the United States was once again at war, this time on foreign soil. People were driving automobiles, women were gradually getting the vote, the telephone was commonplace, and railroads ran all over the country. But the buffalo was almost extinct, the American Indians were confined to reservations, and the Wild West show was no more.

Bill became Buffalo Bill as a way to support his family. He entered the public eye as a young man with long hair—the fashion of the time. He once said that if he ever were to cut it, he'd never make another nickel. When he was a much older man and started losing his hair, he wore a wig, because his long hair was so much a part of his image. So were the clothes he wore—his Stetson hat, his fringed jacket and leather boots. Western clothing, still stylish today, was never more glamorous than it was in the Wild West show.

From his childhood onward, Bill had always been a fair person, and when he became famous and influential he did some things that many others considered to be radical for the times. Women in his show who did the same work as men received the same pay. When questioned about this, Bill pointed out to critics that the cowgirls with his show were every bit as skillful as the cowboys.

Many of the Native Americans in his show had their families with them, and if these family members appeared in the show in any capacity, they were paid, including the children. Also, in the show's program in 1899, Bill urged his audience to support giving women the vote. He

Cowgirls did the same work as men—while wearing skirts. Bill featured their roping and riding skills in the Wild West show. Called "Buffalo Gals," several even became famous.

told a reporter that he believed strongly in women's rights because of his love for his mother.

With the Wild West show, Bill created a form of entertainment that was the precursor of the rodeo and the Hollywood Western. Others tried to copy him, but for thirty years his show was both the original and the best.

THE PERSONAL BILL CODY

Bill adored all children. Wherever the show went, he made sure that orphaned or poor children got free tickets. He was devoted to his own children and hated being parted from them while he traveled with the show. He returned to the family home in North Platte, Nebraska, to be with them whenever he could. Occasionally the children and Louisa traveled with him, but Louisa preferred staying home.

Bill had a soft spot for all children. He liked to have his own children travel with him whenever possible.

The greatest sorrows of his life were the deaths of three of his four children. His son and middle daughter died of illnesses during childhood. His eldest daughter died of illness in her twenties, leaving only the youngest daughter, Irma, to survive her father.

Bill was close to his sisters all of his life. He turned to Julia for advice and support and wrote her frequent letters, often addressing her as "darling sister." The sisters and their families all relied on him financially, and he was generous to a fault, just as he was with countless charities and his legions of friends.

He was interested in making money but never in managing it. He made huge sums and he lost huge sums, investing in risky schemes that always seemed to fail. He was in financial trouble at the end of his life, though by then he had lived for many years as a wealthy man.

During much of his adult life, Bill struggled with a drinking problem. He drank because it was considered manly—and he was the most manly of men. He also drank for enjoyment, and sometimes he drank because he was overwhelmed with all of his responsibilities. He was able to stop drinking for the last fifteen years of his life.

When he died in 1917, he was buried just outside Denver, on Lookout Mountain. He had chosen the spot himself, telling his wife, "You can look down on four states there." Louisa died in 1921 and was buried next to him.

BILL CODY AND CONSERVATION

Even as he celebrated his vision of the Old West, Bill had his eye on the New West, for he was deeply committed to the responsible development of western lands. Because of this, Buffalo Bill Dam in Wyoming was named for him. Like his father before him, he helped start a town. His was Cody, Wyoming, close to the east entrance of Yellowstone National Park. Bill loved Yellowstone and wanted to make it easier for more people to visit it. His town helped, and so did President Theodore Roosevelt, for Bill persuaded him to support the building of a highway from Cody into the park. "I would take chances on building a road into the middle of eternity on his statement," said Roosevelt of his good friend Bill Cody.

BILL CODY AND THE AMERICAN INDIAN

During Bill's lifetime, Native Americans were in a battle for survival against whites and the US government. Bill felt that the tribes should give way to white settlement and accept US government rule. But he didn't like the way they were treated.

Bill and Sitting Bull posed for this publicity photo in 1885. Bill wrote of the chief, "In war [I was] his bitter opponent, in peace he won my friendship and sympathy."

He felt they had been humiliated, beaten, and driven onto reservations. The government did not allow them to practice their ceremonial dances or to use bows and arrows. They were expected to learn English and to think, act, and dress like whites.

Bill never apologized for featuring them in his show and for treating them well. He honored their superior skills as warriors and as horsemen. In every show they demonstrated their hunting skills and performed their war dances. They created their own village of tepees wherever the show went, allowing curious visitors to learn how they had once lived on the plains and prairies of America before they were driven off their land. In celebrating their culture in the Wild West show, Bill gave them back some of their dignity.

PEOPLE AND PLACES
YOU'VE MET IN THIS BOOK

John Brown left Kansas in 1859, going east to raise money from abolitionists to help finance the great slave rebellion he hoped to incite. In need of weapons, he planned a raid on the federal arsenal at Harpers Ferry, West Virginia. The night of October 16, 1859, Brown and twenty-two men, including three of his sons and several freed slaves, took over the Harpers Ferry armory, expecting local slaves to rise up and support them. This did not happen, and by the following morning federal militia surrounded the armory. Men on both sides were killed in the ensuing standoff. The government sent Colonel Robert E. Lee and a company of marines to end it. Brown was seriously injured before he was captured. He was tried, found guilty of treason, and hanged.

In death, Brown was honored as a martyr to the cause of

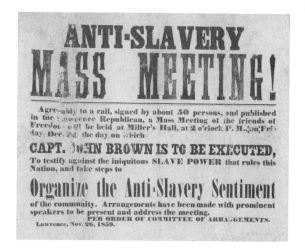

A meeting in Lawrence on the day of John Brown's execution helped unite anti-slavery groups.

slavery. Harriet Tubman, a freed slave and a leading activist in the Underground Railroad, said that Brown was the true emancipator of her people, and the African-American abolitionist Frederick Douglass wrote in 1861, "If we look over the dates, places and men, for which this honor is claimed, we shall find that not Carolina, but Virginia—not Fort Sumter, but Harper's Ferry and the arsenal—not Col. Anderson, but John Brown began the war that ended American slavery and made this a free Republic."

But Brown's legacy is mixed. In December 1859, the then–presidential candidate Abraham Lincoln visited Leavenworth, Kansas. He told an audience on the day after Brown's execution that while

he admired Brown's courage, it could not excuse his use of violence and bloodshed.

Charles Robinson and **Jim Lane** despised each other until Lane's death. Though always dogged by rumors of graft and corruption, Lane was elected by Kansans to the United States Senate in January 1865. Six months later, at age fifty-two, he suffered a mental collapse and killed himself. Robinson lived to the age of seventy-six, dying in 1894. Often referred to as the father of Kansas, he served as both state senator and governor and remained active in local politics well into old age.

When Private Billy Cody, dressed as a Tennessee country boy, located the Confederate forces of **General Nathan Bedford Forrest**, the stage was set for the defeat of one of the South's best leaders. A Tennessee native, Forrest was born poor and had little education, yet he became one of the wealthiest men in the South, making his fortune as a planter and a slave trader. He had no military experience when the war began but rose through the ranks. He had twenty-nine horses shot out from under him and was wounded four times. After the war he was part of the Ku Klux Klan and was possibly its first grand wizard.

Buffalo Bill's famous friend **Wild Bill** was born James Butler Hickok in Illinois in 1837. When he was twenty he homesteaded a claim in what is now Lenexa, Kansas, and was one of the Jayhawker Red Legs during the Border War. In spite of his nickname, Wild Bill was courteous and soft-spoken. He was also a superb marksman and he earned a reputation as a gunfighter. After his Civil War service he worked as an army scout, tried a few months on the stage with Buffalo Bill, and served as a lawman in several Kansas towns. When vision problems forced him out of the law business, he headed to the Dakota Territory to

try his luck in the goldfields. He was playing poker in the town of Deadwood when he was fatally shot in the back by a man holding a grudge against him. He was thirty-nine.

William Clarke Quantrill and his men reached Missouri

safely after their raid on Lawrence. But Union forces were determined to bring Quantrill to justice, and from then on he was a hunted man. Quantrill and his followers killed and looted wherever they went. They were ambushed by federal soldiers in Kentucky a month after the South's

surrender in 1865. Quantrill was wounded and died in custody several weeks later. He was twenty-eight.

KANSAS DURING AND AFTER THE WAR

Although Kansas had become a state only a few months before the start of the Civil War, it supplied 20,000 soldiers for the Union cause, including five regiments of African-Americans and three of Native Americans. More than 8,500 Kansas soldiers

African-American soldiers in Kansas were mobilized at Fort Leavenworth. Several companies are shown here at the end of the war.

died. Many people had questioned the ability of African-Americans to fight, but they were proved wrong. An officer wrote of the First Kansas Colored Infantry, "They fought like veterans . . . their line unbroken. . . . Their coolness and bravery I have never seen surpassed."

When the war ended in April 1865, Kansas faced several major challenges. Governor Samuel J. Crawford noted, "We had nothing with which to set up housekeeping except the State Seal, a lease on some leaky buildings, and quite an assortment of bills payable." But the motto on the State Seal was *ad astra per aspera*—to the stars through difficulties—and Crawford also proclaimed that "Kansas is free, and now offers to the immigrant a home unsurpassed in beauty, richness, and fertility." During the next decade more than two dozen colleges and universities were established in Kansas, helping to build the foundation of a great state.

In the years after the Civil War, African-Americans in the South realized that they were never going to be treated as equals. Indeed, as the oppressive Jim Crow laws assured that they would remain second-class citizens, more and more began to migrate north. About 20,000 settled in Kansas, because it had been the home of John Brown and a battleground in the fight against slavery. Known as Exodusters, many of these Southern emigrants became homesteaders—realizing an opportunity that they did not have in the South to own land.

MISSOURI: A DIVIDED STATE

In the first year of the Civil War, forty-five percent of the war's casualties occurred in Missouri. Guerrilla warfare took a heavy toll even several years after the war, and when the conflict was finally over, nearly 30,000 Missouri civilians were dead. Because of divided loyalties, Missourians sometimes ended up in battle against each other, as they did at the siege of Vicksburg.

Missouri was the setting of the first major Civil War battle west of the Mississippi—at Wilson's Creek—and the largest battle west of the Mississippi: the Battle of Westport in Kansas City. General Price's loss at Westport forecasted the South's defeat.

At the end of the war the state was in shambles, for Union troops had pillaged and burned the land everywhere. Hardest hit was the area along the border with Kansas known as the Burnt District. It was destroyed as a result of General Order Number 11, issued by the Union command in retribution for Quantrill's raid on Lawrence. It gave civilians fifteen days to leave before Kansas cavalry burned their homes. Soldiers and civilians returning after the war found charred ruins where once their homes had stood. In despair, many Missourians left forever, for with their farms destroyed they could not support themselves. A few former Confederates became outlaws, including Frank and Jesse James and Cole Younger and his brothers. Lawlessness was an ongoing problem for years.

THE TIGER, THE JAYHAWK, AND THE BORDER WAR

It's estimated that by the end of the Civil War, 27,000 civilians had died in the border warfare between Kansas and Missouri. In an odd way, the contention between the two states continues today, although it is good-natured. Competition between the University of Kansas (KU) and the University of Missouri (MU) has long been referred to as the Border War, perpetuating a rivalry, albeit mostly in sports, between the two states.

MU was founded in 1839 in Columbia, Missouri, and was the first public university west of the Mississippi. Legend has it that during the Civil War when Confederate guerillas threatened pro-Union Columbia, the home guard called themselves the Missouri Tigers to scare off would-be invaders. Later the college football team took the name to honor the town's defenders, and eventually the tiger became the university's mascot.

KU borrowed the name of the mythical bird that during the Border War had inspired the infamous Jayhawkers, who helped defend Kansas from Missouri Bushwhackers (but who also inflicted much suffering on Missouri citizens in their raids across the border). Today the Jayhawk is the proud symbol of the university founded on the summit of Mount Oread in Lawrence in 1865, at the end of the Civil War.

TRACES OF THE BORDER WAR TODAY

According to most history books, the Civil War officially began when Confederate forces fired on Union-held Fort

Sumter in Charleston Harbor on April 12, 1861. But in actuality it had been underway in Bleeding Kansas since 1854.

Visitors to eastern Kansas and western Missouri will find many places of interest associated with the Border War and the Civil War. See www.civilwartraveler.com, then click on "Kansas" and "Missouri" for information about key places to visit. At www.free-domsfrontier.org you can learn more about the people and the history of the Border War.

If you have an opportunity to visit Leavenworth, Kansas, you will discover a picturesque riverfront town with lovely historic homes. At nearby Fort Leavenworth you will see the oldest working fort west of the Mississippi. Of special interest are the Frontier Army Museum and the Buffalo Soldier Monument. Several miles from the fort is the Salt Creek Valley, where the Codys had their farm. You will immediately understand why they chose this place as their home and why Billy Cody called it "the most beautiful valley I had ever seen."

After a grasshopper infestation in 1870, the citizens of Grasshopper Falls changed the town's name to Valley Falls. Located twenty-five miles from Topeka, it now has a population of 1,100 residents. The town's history mentions Isaac Cody and his sawmill and notes that Wild Bill Hickok came there once on business and danced with the local ladies at a social gathering. Violence between pro- and anti-slave factions brought much hardship to the area before and during the Civil War. The town was rebuilt after it was burned and pillaged by border ruffians.

In Lecompton, the first capital of Kansas Territory, several historic buildings help illuminate the story of the Border War. The pro-slave Lecompton Constitution was written and voted on at Constitution Hall, a National Historical Landmark.

Sara Robinson sketched Massachusetts Street after the massacre. The phoenix became the Lawrence symbol: like the mythological bird, the town rose from the ashes to begin again.

Lawrence rose from the ashes after Quantrill's raid and grew rapidly.

Today it is a thriving city with a population nearing one hundred thousand. The best view in town is from the top of Mount Oread on the campus of the University of Kansas. A walk down Massachusetts Street to the Eldridge Hotel is a walk through history, for this was Quantrill's path. In Old West Lawrence, visitors can see several fine old houses on Louisiana and

Tennessee Streets that survived Quantrill. A map available on-line shows various markers around the city related to the raid. For more information, go to www.visitlawrence.com/history/civil-war. Lawrence is also home to Haskell Indian Nations University, founded in 1884. It is the only four-year Indian university in the United States. One hundred and fifty tribes are represented in its student body.

Kansas City began in the historic section of the town known as Westport. The three-day Battle of Westport was centered in nearby Loose Park, where historical markers explain how the events unfolded. At the time, Wornall Road, which borders the park's eastern side, was called Bloody Lane because Confederate ambulances used it to carry the wounded to a hospital set up at the elegant John Wornall House. When the Confederates retreated, the Yankees took it over for use as a Union hospital. Visitors can learn about the area's history at the Westport Historical Society (www.westporthistorical.com) and at the Wornall House Museum (www.wornallhouse.org).

At www.ushistory.org, click on "Bleeding Kansas" for more information about events that affected eastern Kansas during the Border War.

BUFFALO BILL COUNTRY

Bill had a large cattle ranch at North Platte, Nebraska. He considered it his permanent home and called it Scout's Rest Ranch. Today it is the Buffalo Bill Ranch State Historical Park. Visitors can camp in the park, enjoy many exhibits, and tour the home, which has been restored to look as it did when Bill lived there. For more information, go to visitnorthplatte.com/attraction/buffalo-bill-state-historical-park/.

LeClaire, Iowa, Bill's birthplace, has its own Buffalo Bill Museum, which features exhibits on Bill's life and Iowa history. See www.buffalobillmuseumleclaire.com.

In Cody, Wyoming, visitors feel Bill's presence everywhere, and especially at the Irma Hotel, founded by Bill and named for his youngest daughter. No trip to Cody would be complete without enjoying a meal in the Irma's dining room, which looks much as it did when it opened in 1902. See www.irmahotel.com for more information.

The showpiece of Cody is the Buffalo Bill Center of the West, which houses Western art and artifacts, and extensive displays on Native American tribes and on Buffalo Bill. The center is also home to the Buffalo Bill archives and the McCracken Research Library to

The IRMA,
Buffalo Bill's Hotel in the Rockies.
F.J. Hiscock Photo Cody Wyo. 1908.

Bill spared no expense when he built the grand Irma Hotel in Cody. Five hundred guests attended its official opening in 1902.

Advance the Study of the American West. This fine museum is sometimes referred to as the Smithsonian of the West. For more information, visit www.centerofthewest.org.

Just outside Cody is the Buffalo Bill Dam and Buffalo Bill State Park. Bill was a devoted conservationist and an advocate for the dam on the Shoshone River. It helps irrigate the Bighorn Basin, allowing agriculture to flourish on what was once arid land.

At Colorado's Lookout Mountain, visitors can see Bill Cody's grave and explore the nearby Buffalo Bill Museum. To learn more about Bill's life and the Wild West show, see www.buffalobill.org.

AUTHOR'S NOTE

———◆•◆———

I grew up in Nebraska, and I always thought that Buffalo Bill Cody did, too. I knew he had owned a ranch in North Platte that had become a state park, and that a Nebraska rodeo and other events were named for him. I didn't know much about him, except that I associated his name with his Wild West show.

So when I heard about him in London when I was visiting there, I was surprised. I had taken a walking tour of Brompton Cemetery, which dates back to the Victorian era and is the final resting place of many well-known people. Our guide stopped at a simple stone cross with the carving of a wolf on it. He told us that this had been the grave of Lone Wolf, a Sioux chief who had died of pneumonia when he was with Buffalo Bill's Wild West show on its second visit to England in 1892. Because of the difficulties of shipping the chief's body back to his family, they requested that he be buried in London, so Buffalo Bill purchased the plot for him. The cross had stayed in place ever since, even after the chief's remains were returned to his

Oglala Sioux descendants for burial in 1997. The guide talked at length about Buffalo Bill and his Wild West show—how it came to London several times, how Queen Victoria was a huge fan, and that it was Buffalo Bill who had introduced Europeans to real Indians and to the American West.

Lone Wolf (far right) posed in 1875 with Buffalo Bill and seven other Native American chiefs in the show. To Bill's left are Lakota Sioux, and to his right are Pawnees.

As impressed as I was to learn that this native Nebraskan had been an international superstar, an even bigger surprise awaited me in eastern Kansas, where I now live.

I had begun researching this book, planning that it would tell the story of Bleeding Kansas and its border war with Missouri during the six years preceding the Civil War. I needed a young person to anchor my story—a boy or girl through whose eyes my readers would experience this history—just as I have done with all my books. When Bob Spear, a bookseller and a historian in Leavenworth, Kansas, suggested Buffalo Bill Cody, I responded that he was a Nebraskan. No, Bob said, he grew up near Leavenworth, in the thick of the Border War. Nebraskans claim him because his adult home was there, but Iowans also claim him because he was born there; Coloradoans claim him because he's buried there, and folks in his beloved Wyoming claim him because he founded the town of Cody and spent lots of time there. During Buffalo Bill's lifetime, as I soon learned, he was a soldier, scout, guide, buffalo hunter, entrepreneur and businessman, generous philanthropist, supporter of women's rights, both foe and friend to the American Indian, environmentalist, founder of the Wild West show, and one of the most famous people in the world.

But was he the best central character for my book? I read several accounts of his childhood, when he was known as Billy Cody, and I knew I'd found my anchor.

Just as most Americans know about the Civil War but not its history here on the Kansas-Missouri border, they know about Buffalo Bill the showman but not about his childhood. His story as it intertwines with Bleeding Kansas reveals yet again that war can be as threatening for civilians as it is for soldiers. When children and their families are inevitably caught up in the hostilities, some pay the ultimate price. This is as true today as it was for Billy Cody in those dramatic years that served as prelude to the Civil War.

—ANDREA WARREN

ACKNOWLEDGMENTS

———◆·◆———

I am grateful to many people who have assisted me with research, ideas, editing, and encouragement in bringing this book to life. Bob Spear at the Book Barn in Leavenworth first directed my attention to Buffalo Bill, and both he and his wife, Barbara, offered me warm support. Patti Hoddinott was with me when we discovered Lone Wolf's grave in London and has taken a lively interest in every Buffalo Bill moment of my life since then; Sandy Lamb took the trip west with me to explore Bill's beloved Wyoming. Mary Robinson, the director of the McCracken Research Library at the Buffalo Bill Center of the West in Cody, and her staff welcomed me to the library and assisted me in my research there. The staff at Corinth Public Library near my home in Prairie Village, Kansas, cheerfully accommodated my extensive and repeated requests for research materials. My agent, Regina Ryan, encouraged me to pursue this story from the moment I told her about Buffalo Bill. I have worked with my editor, Melanie Kroupa, on two other books, and I am delighted that we could collaborate on this one, too. Barbara Bartocci guided me to Leavenworth, Fort Leavenworth, and the beautiful Salt Creek Valley so I could see for myself where Billy Cody and his family lived and worked. I am, as always, indebted to Barbara and to Deborah Shouse for their patience and skill in helping me plod through the hard work of shaping the text. Writing can be lonely work, but a supportive writers' community can bring sunlight to darkness, and I am blessed.

MORE ABOUT BUFFALO BILL
AND HIS TIMES

———◆·◆———

BOOKS

Readers can learn more about Bill Cody in *Buffalo Bill: Scout, Showman, Visionary*, by Steve Friesen (Golden, CO: Fulcrum Publishing, 2010), a book rich in both story and photos. In it, readers will also get to see many photos of Cody's personal belongings, including his gun and saddle.

Cowboy: An Album, by Linda Granfield (New York: Ticknor & Fields, 1994) is a well-illustrated book that will help readers understand the everyday life Billy Cody lived on the westward trails.

The Civil War in Kansas: Ten Years of Turmoil, by Debra Goodrich Bisel (Charleston, SC: The History Press, 2012) is a basic book about what happened in Kansas during the Border War and the Civil War that followed it.

In *John Brown: His Fight for Freedom*, by John Hendrix (New York: Harry N. Abrams, 2009), young readers will find out more about the radical abolitionist and his quest to free the slaves.

Ride with the Devil (originally titled *Woe to Live On*), by Daniel Woodrell (New York: Pocket Books, 1987) is an excellent fast-paced novel about the Border War for older and adult readers. It's told from the perspective of Missourians, some becoming Bushwhackers who participated in Quantrill's raid on Lawrence.

They're Off! The Story of the Pony Express, by Cheryl Harness (New York: Simon & Schuster Books for Young Readers, 2002) will thrill readers with its story of how the Pony Express operated and the boy riders who made it possible.

Younger readers will discover the basics about the Underground Railroad and its importance in freeing slaves in *If You Traveled on the Underground Railroad*, by Ellen Levine (New York: Scholastic, 1993).

For a behind-the-scenes look at Annie Oakley and the other women who traveled with Buffalo Bill's Wild West, readers will enjoy *Buffalo Gals: Women of Buffalo Bill's Wild West Show*, by Chris Enss (Guilford, CT: Globe Pequot, 2005).

MOVIES

*L*incoln (directed by Steven Spielberg and starring Daniel Day-Lewis as Abraham Lincoln). This 2012 award-winning movie addresses the President's struggle near the end of the Civil War to get Congress to enact a constitutional amendment to end slavery.

Ride with the Devil (directed by Ang Lee and starring Tobey Maguire). This 1999 film based on Daniel Woodrell's novel is set along the Missouri-Kansas border prior to and during the Civil War, it tells the story of a small band of Bushwhackers. Included is an enactment of Quantrill's Raid on Lawrence.

DOCUMENTARIES

*B*ad Blood. Using a multimedia approach, this documentary includes historical photos, paintings, quotes from historians and eyewitnesses, and music to enhance actors recreating many of the major incidents that occurred in Kansas and Missouri.

Buffalo Bill. Produced for the PBS series *American Experience* in 2008, this documentary includes archival photos and video of

Buffalo Bill and his Wild West show. Of special interest is historical footage of American Indian participants and an exploration of Buffalo Bill's relationship with them, including the Sioux chief Sitting Bull, who spent one season with the show.

Buffalo Bill Cody. This 2010 documentary features extensive archival footage of the Wild West show. A rare piece of footage shows Buffalo Bill conversing in sign language.

The Great Indian Wars, 1540–1890. This five-part series explores Native American history and the 350-year conflict with whites that culminated with the Battle of Wounded Knee.

Touched by Fire: Bleeding Kansas. This documentary covers John Brown's pivotal role in the fight over slavery in Kansas Territory and includes reenactments of key scenes in Brown's struggle to free the slaves.

RESEARCHING THIS BOOK

Imagining scenes set in places I've never been can be difficult, but working on this book has been different, for I am acquainted with the landscape of Bill Cody's life. Interestingly, when I taught in London for several months, I lived in the area known as Earl's Court—the very location where the Wild West show was performed. More important, I have lived most of my life in the Midwest, the majority of it in eastern Kansas, close to the Missouri border where Bill grew to adulthood. My home is mere blocks from Loose Park, which was part of the Battle of Westport. I lived for ten years in Lawrence, Kansas, home of the abolitionists, the free-staters, the Underground Railroad, and Quantrill's raid. I grew up in Nebraska and know well the terrain along the wide, shallow Platte River leading to Fort Kearny. I've been out West numerous times, including a trip to the Valley of the Great Salt Lake.

While writing this book, I journeyed to Cody, Wyoming, to experience the town that Bill founded and to conduct research in the archives of the great museum there, the Buffalo Bill Center of the West. I read letters that Bill and his family wrote to each other, studied original family photos and Wild West show photos, and perused long-ago newspaper clippings. In the museum itself, I saw clothing and possessions that had belonged to Bill, and I found the fine displays, paintings, and photographs throughout the museum to be both inspiring and informative in helping me bring alive Bill's story. In studying the details of that life, the three versions he wrote about himself, and his sister Julia's book about him, were especially valuable.

In addition to the sources listed in the Bibliography, I found these books especially helpful: *Buffalo Bill: Scout, Showman, Visionary*, by Steve Friesen; *The Story of the Lawrence Massacre*, by Thomas Goodrich; and *The Lives and Legends of Buffalo Bill*, by Don Russell.

NOTES

CHAPTER 1: LOSING SAM

3　"My brother was a great favorite": Cody, *Life of Hon. William F. Cody*, p. 23.

3　"so affected in health": Wetmore, *Last of the Great Scouts*, chapter 1.

5　"My Father had determined to take up a claim": Cody, *An Autobiography*, chapter 1.

CHAPTER 2: ON THE ROAD TO KANSAS

8　"I was second in command": Cody, *An Autobiography*, chapter 1.

10　"I've heard of dogs saving children": Wetmore, *Last of the Great Scouts*, chapter 1.

11　"a genuine child of nature": Leonard and Goodman, *Buffalo Bill*, p. 38.

11　"There was something new to be seen": Cody, *Life of Hon. William F. Cody*, p. 24.

CHAPTER 3: SLAVERY BECOMES REAL

13　"a large and handsome brick residence": Cody, *Life of Hon. William F. Cody*, p. 28.

13　"All of the servants were Negro slaves": Leonard and Goodman, *Buffalo Bill*, p. 43.

16　"there was great rejoicing": Ibid., p. 44.

16　"could not become accustomed": Ibid., p. 45.

CHAPTER 4: BILLY VISITS FORT LEAVENWORTH

21　"I shall never forget the thrill": Cody, *An Autobiography*, chapter 1.

21　"About the post were men dressed all in buckskin": Ibid.

22　"Cavalry were engaged in saber drills": Ibid.

22　"These drills were no fancy dress parades": Ibid.

22　"From its summit we had a view": Cody, *Life of Hon. William F. Cody*, p. 31.

CHAPTER 5: ARRIVING IN THE PROMISED LAND

24　"A large number of the wagons": Cody, *Life of Hon. William F. Cody*, p.32.

(CHAPTER 5: ARRIVING IN THE PROMISED LAND, CON'T.)

24   "Perhaps a hundred men": Ibid., p. 33.

25   "was very limited": Ibid., p. 21.

25   "The Kickapoo were very friendly": Ibid., p. 35.

26   "I made up my mind that I was going to ride": Cody, *An Autobiography*, chapter 1.

27   "Boys are always hungry": Ibid.

27   "He had a long talk with father": Cody, *Life of Hon. William F. Cody*, p. 38.

27   "Neither Father nor myself": Ibid., p. 39.

27   "With very little trouble": Cody, *An Autobiography*, chapter 1.

28   "My ambition . . . was to become": Cody, *Life of Hon. William F. Cody*, p. 40.

28   "With Father's consent": Ibid., p. 41.

29   "Everything that he did": Ibid.

29   "That same day": Ibid., p. 42.

29   "became very friendly": Ibid., p. 43.

30   "The Indians roasted a steer": Leonard and Goodman, *Buffalo Bill*, p. 54.

30   "Mother made several large boilers": Cody, *Life of Hon. William F. Cody*, p. 43.

30   "In the lands to the north and west": Leonard and Goodman, *Buffalo Bill*, p. 55.

CHAPTER 6: AT HOME IN THE VALLEY

32   "the Codys had the honor": Leonard and Goodman, *Buffalo Bill*, p. 50.

33   "Some of these Missourians": Ibid., p. 56.

35   "He minded his own business": *Cody, An Autobiography*, chapter 1.

36   "On Saturday night the squaws visited": Leonard and Goodman, *Buffalo Bill*, p. 54.

38   "[Mr. Russell] seemed to take a considerable interest": Cody, *Life and Adventures*, chapter 1.

CHAPTER 7: ISAAC CODY'S BLOODY TRAIL

40   "for a time it was taken for granted": Cody, *An Autobiography*, chapter 1.

40   "He was never at any pains": Ibid.

40   "We saw a crowd of drunken horsemen": Ibid.

41   "By this time more than a dozen men": Ibid.

41   "I am not ashamed of my views": Ibid.

(CHAPTER 7: ISAAC CODY'S BLOODY TRAIL, CON'T)

41   "a wild yell of derision": Ibid.

41   "jumped up on the box": Ibid.

42   "Look out, [you'll] stab the kid!" Ibid.

42   "I believed he was mortally wounded": Ibid.

43   "Mother nursed Father carefully": Ibid.

43   "A Mr. Cody, a noisy abolitionist": Warren, *Buffalo Bill's America,* p. 10.

43   "The path over which he was borne by wagon": Leonard and Goodman, *Buffalo Bill,* p. 58.

44   "He was threatened with death by hanging": Cody, *Life and Adventures,* chapter 1.

44   "saw some men racing along the stacks": Leonard and Goodman, *Buffalo Bill,* p. 58.

44   "months of effort went up in smoke": Ibid.

45   "carrying a water pail": Ibid.

45   "Mother very truthfully told them": Cody, *Life of Hon. William F. Cody,* p. 50.

46   "I am sure if they had captured Father": Ibid.

46   "My first real work as a scout": Leonard and Goodman, *Buffalo Bill,* p. 58.

47   "None of us knew whether we should ever again": Wetmore, *Last of the Great Scouts,* chapter 3.

CHAPTER 8: PRO-SLAVE OR FREE STATE?

48   "I have my rifle, revolver, and pistol": Gilmore, *Civil War on the Missouri-Kansas Border,* p. 58.

49   "this same punishment we will award": Sell and Weybright, *Buffalo Bill and the Wild West,* p. 12.

51   "Now, I knew something about a gun": Cody, *An Autobiography,* chapter 1.

51   "I'm going to finish up the job": Ibid.

51   "Father could be of no service to us": Ibid.

52   "Mother had made up her mind": Cody, *Life of Hon. William F. Cody,* p. 54.

53   "could not assist us much": Ibid., p. 55.

53   "quiet presence": Leonard and Goodman, *Buffalo Bill,* p. 71.

54   "Again an army of Missourians invaded Kansas": Ibid., p. 61.

CHAPTER 9: BILLY SOUNDS THE ALARM

57 "'Billy, my boy,' said Russell": Cody, *Life and Adventures,* chapter 1.

57 "I accepted the offer": Ibid.

57 "She refused to let me go": Ibid.

57 "stole away and walked": Ibid.

59 "I put the bright silver coins into a sack": Ibid.

61 "two legislatures, each refusing to accept": Leonard and Goodman, *Buffalo Bill,* p. 65.

62 "Not a day or night went by": Ibid., p. 68.

63 "the little school at home": Cody, *Life and Adventures,* chapter 1.

63 "Miss Lyons carried on the work of the school": Leonard and Goodman, *Buffalo Bill,* p. 63.

64 "That's Cody's boy!" Wetmore, *Last of the Great Scouts,* chapter 4.

64 "A pistol shot, to terrify me into obedience": Cody, *An Autobiography,* chapter 1.

64 "I instantly started my pony on a run": Cody, *Life of Hon. William F. Cody,* p. 52.

64 "I urged Prince to his utmost speed": Ibid.

64 "I led my pursuers on a lively chase": Ibid.

CHAPTER 10: BILLY MEETS THE ABOLITIONISTS

67 "Lawrence is the commercial, literary, and political center": Goodrich, *Bloody Dawn,* p. 47.

71 "We had now been reduced to utter destitution": Cody, *An Autobiography,* chapter 1.

71 "Hardly a day passed": Cody, *Life and Adventures,* chapter 1.

71 "Govern Kansas! You might as well attempt to govern": Nichols, *Bleeding Kansas,* p. 139.

CHAPTER 11: JOHN BROWN'S WAR IN KANSAS

75 "as the flames hissed and crackled": Pickett, *Voices of the Past,* p. 120.

76 "put spurs to our horses": Cody, *Life of Hon. William F. Cody,* p. 29.

77 "Those were heart-rending days for my young mother": Stratton, *Pioneer Women,* p. 234.

(CHAPTER 11: JOHN BROWN'S WAR IN KANSAS, CON'T)

77   "I went to take Old Brown": Gilmore, *Civil War on the Missouri-Kansas Border*, p. 76.

78   "before they left, my mother and I got up": Stratton, *Pioneer Women*, p. 239.

CHAPTER 12: FATHER

79   "Men were shot down in their homes": Cody, *Life and Adventures*, chapter 1.

81   "After taking every horse and wagon": Stratton, *Pioneer Women*, p. 243.

81   "'We will not kill women and children'": Ibid.

81   "I have only a short time to live": *John Brown and Bleeding Kansas*, inside cover.

82   "With the help of John Brown": Cody, *An Autobiography*, chapter 1.

82   "addressed the delegates": Leonard and Goodman, *Buffalo Bill*, p. 70.

82   "We looked out": Cody, *Life of Hon. William F. Cody*, p. 57.

84   "a joyous time": Leonard and Goodman, *Buffalo Bill*, p. 71.

85   "Though worn by work and worry": Ibid., p. 72.

85   "The wound inflicted by Dunn": Cody, *An Autobiography*, chapter 1.

CHAPTER 13: BILLY THE HERO

86   "I was eleven years old": Cody, *An Autobiography*, chapter 1.

86   "I determined to follow the plains": Cody, *Life of Hon. William F. Cody*, p. 69.

86   "At this sorrowful period": Wetmore, *Last of the Great Scouts*, chapter 5.

89   "With forty dollars a month": Cody, *An Autobiography*, chapter 1.

89   "With tears in our eyes": Wetmore, *Last of the Great Scouts*, chapter 5.

90   "The trip [was] full of excitement": Cody, *An Autobiography*, chapter 1.

91   "there was a sharp Bang!" Ibid.

91   "Indians! They've shot the herders": Ibid.

92   "It was a long [exhausting] journey": Ibid.

92   "I was not only overcome with astonishment": Cody, *Life and Adventures*, chapter 1.

92   "we pushed on": Cody, *An Autobiography*, chapter 1.

92   "it made me the envy of all the boys": Ibid.

92   "I feel very much elated": Cody, *Life and Adventures*, chapter 1.

93   "Billy walked around for days": Leonard and Goodman, *Buffalo Bill*, p. 83.

93   "[Mother] rushed Billy off to the bathroom": Ibid., p. 80.

CHAPTER 14: TROUBLE WITH THE MORMONS

94　"lead a life on the Plains": Cody, *An Autobiography*, chapter 1.

95　"You seem to have a reputation": Ibid.

97　"'We do not want to fight the United States'": Settle and Lund, *War Drums and Wagon Wheels*, p. 58.

97　"I am ordered there": Ibid., p. 61.

97　"Our long train, twenty-five wagons": Cody, *An Autobiography*, chapter 1.

99　"took particular delight in bullying": Cody, *Life of Hon. William F. Cody*, p. 82.

100　"If you ever again lay a hand on that boy": Ibid., p. 83.

100　"We beat off the attacks": Cody, *An Autobiography*, chapter 1.

100　"They were all armed": Cody, *Life and Adventures*, chapter 1.

100　"'I'll trouble you for your six-shooters'": Ibid.

101　"Simpson was a brave man": Cody, *An Autobiography*, chapter 1.

101　"They watched us depart": Ibid.

102　"The smoke [rolled] up in dense clouds": Cody, *Life and Adventures*, chapter 1.

102　"impressed me as a rather fresh": Russell, *Lives and Legends of Buffalo Bill*, p. 35.

104　"The first to welcome me was my old dog Turk": Cody, *An Autobiography*, chapter 1.

CHAPTER 15: BILLY AND THE INDIANS

105　"fell in ringlets over his shoulders": Leonard and Goodman, *Buffalo Bill*, p. 100.

106　"'Julia,' Billy said, 'Wild Bill is my best friend'": Ibid., p. 101.

106　"always referred to the Salt Creek Valley house": Ibid.

107　"had become the most famous meeting-place": Cody, *An Autobiography*, chapter 1.

108　"a small, dapper, quiet man": Ibid.

108　"I used to sit for hours and watch him": Ibid.

108　"I . . . began my education in it with far more interest": Ibid.

108　"My wagon bed became [a] splendid playhouse": Ibid.

109　"Snap! went something": Ibid.

109　"I watched him start off on foot": Ibid.

110　"I had cut twelve of these notches": Ibid.

(CHAPTER 15: BILLY AND THE INDIANS, CON'T.)

110   "The brilliant colors that had been smeared": Ibid.

110   "It was plain from the deference accorded him": Ibid.

110   "He replied that he did": Ibid.

112   "Worse than all these troubles": Ibid.

112   "when I had about given up hope": Ibid.

112   "Harrington had made a trip": Ibid.

112   "as one returned from the dead": Ibid.

113   "had so dulled the memory of my sufferings": Ibid.

CHAPTER 16: BILLY RIDES THE PONY EXPRESS

115   "Wanted: Young, skinny, wiry fellows": frontiertrails.com/oldwest/ponyexpress.htm.

117   "Never before had [the Indians] been followed": Cody, *An Autobiography,* chapter 2.

117   "At our captain's signal": Ibid.

118   "in the usual manner": Cody, *Life of Hon. William F. Cody,* p. 123.

118   "I was returning home empty-handed": Cody, *An Autobiography,* chapter 2.

118   "'A friend and a white man'": Ibid.

118   "Eight of the most villainous-appearing ruffians": Ibid.

119   "I was . . . certain that I had uncovered": Ibid.

120   "Wheeling about, I saw that the other man": Ibid.

120   "knowing that they could make better time": Ibid.

121   "We found a newly made grave": Ibid.

CHAPTER 17: BILLY'S VOLUNTEER WAR

125   "I miss Mr. Cody so much": Leonard and Goodman, *Buffalo Bill,* p. 102.

125   "Many of my boyhood friends were enlisting": Cody, *An Autobiography,* chapter 2.

126   "If our towns and settlements are laid waste by fire": Goodrich, *Bloody Dawn,* p. 60.

127   "As the sun went down": Ibid., p. 59.

127   "like our family, [had] lost everything": Cody, *Life and Adventures,* chapter 5.

(CHAPTER 17: BILLY'S VOLUNTEER WAR, CON'T.)

127 "the inhabitants must all be secessionists": Russell, *Lives and Legends of Buffalo Bill*, p. 56.

127 "This action may look . . . like horse-stealing": Cody, *Life and Adventures*, chapter 5.

128 "We continued to make similar raids on the Missourians": Russell, *Lives and Legends of Buffalo Bill*, p. 57.

128 "My mother, upon learning that I was engaged": Cody, *Life and Adventures*, chapter 5.

CHAPTER 18: BILLY JOINS THE RED LEGS

131 "I felt I could join without breaking my promise": Cody, *An Autobiography*, chapter 2.

131 "We had plenty to do": Ibid.

131 "The Red Legs are desolating the country": Warren, *Buffalo Bill's America*, p. 34.

132 "a full recital of their deeds": Gilmore, *Civil War on the Missouri-Kansas Border*, p. 162.

132 "the Red-Leggers were proud": Leonard and Goodman, *Buffalo Bill*, p. 129.

133 "We were the biggest gang of thieves on record": Gilmore, *Civil War on the Missouri-Kansas Border*, p. 160.

133 "we had many a lively skirmish with the Bushwhackers": Cody, *Life and Adventures*, chapter 6.

CHAPTER 19: QUANTRILL TAKES REVENGE

135 "Lawrence or hell": Bisel, *Civil War in Kansas*, p. 138.

135 "We all loved him": Gilmore, *Civil War on the Missouri-Kansas Border*, p. 185.

CHAPTER 20: MOTHER

143 "I loved her above all other persons": Cody, *Life of Hon. William F. Cody*, p. 152.

143 "I grew up among some of the roughest men": Friesen, *Buffalo Bill*, p. 12.

144 "a dissolute and reckless life": Cody, *Life and Adventures*, chapter 6.

144 "one day, after having been under the influence": Ibid.

(CHAPTER 20: MOTHER, CON'T.)

144 "Overwhelmed with grief over Mother's death": Wetmore, *Last of the Great Scouts*, chapter 7.

CHAPTER 21: PRIVATE CODY: SCOUT AND SPY

147 "I found many of my old friends": Cody, *An Autobiography*, chapter 2.

147 "was making a great deal of trouble": Ibid.

148 "'You ought to be able to render me valuable service'": Ibid.

149 "'If you are captured'": Ibid.

149 "I was anxious to learn how my disguise was going to work": Ibid.

150 "By acting the part of a rural boy": Ibid.

150 "I now made all speed northward": Ibid.

151 "On the second morning after leaving": Ibid.

151 "My commander was much pleased with my report": Ibid.

151 "if you see anything that I ought to know about": Ibid.

152 "They were greatly alarmed when I came up": Ibid.

152 "But you must leave quickly!": Ibid.

152 "I resolved to do what I could to protect them": Cody, *Life and Adventures*, chapter 6.

152 "By this time the advance guard was coming": Cody, *An Autobiography*, chapter 2.

153 "leaped between them and me": Ibid.

153 "I was most agreeably entertained by the young ladies": Cody, *Life and Adventures*, chapter 6.

154 "A lady and her two daughters were alone there": Cody, *An Autobiography*, chapter 2.

CHAPTER 22: A SOLDIER'S LIFE

157 "You little rascal": Cody, *The Life and Adventures*, chapter 6.

157 "He was greatly surprised and grieved": Ibid.

160 "While we were rounding them up I heard one of them say": Cody, *An Autobiography*, chapter 2.

CHAPTER 23: BECOMING BUFFALO BILL

163 "Buffalo Bill, Buffalo Bill/Never missed": Russell, *Lives and Legends of Buffalo Bill*, p. 90.

CHAPTER 24: BUFFALO BILL'S WILD WEST

175 "noisy, rattling, gunpowder entertainment": Ward, *The West*, p. 375.

178 "I have seen your Wild West Show": Warren, *Buffalo Bill's America*, p. 294.

179 "The defeat of Custer was not a massacre": Sell and Weybright, *Buffalo Bill and the Wild West*, p. 147.

180 "The most interesting episodes of life": Ibid., p. 162.

183 "His heart never left the great West": Ibid., p. 242.

183 "Everything was done to make Cody conceited": Ibid., p. 172.

THE LATER LIFE AND LEGACY OF THE BOY FROM BLEEDING KANSAS

190 "darling sister": Yost, Buffalo Bill, p. 140.

190 "You can look down on four states": Friesen, *Buffalo Bill*, p. 145.

191 "I would take chances on building a road": Russell, *Lives and Legends of Buffalo Bill*, p. 427.

192 "In war [I was] his bitter opponent": Friesen, *Buffalo Bill*, p. 56.

194 "If we look over the dates, places and men": *John Brown and Bleeding Kansas: Prelude to the Civil War*, p. 22.

197 "They fought like veterans": *The Civil War: A Visual History*, p. 227.

197 "We had nothing with which to set up housekeeping": Davis, *Kansas*, p. 94.

197 "Kansas is free, and now offers to the immigrant": Ibid., p. 84.

201 "the most beautiful valley I had ever seen": Cody, *Life of Hon. William F. Cody*, p. 31.

BIBLIOGRAPHY

Bisel, Debra Goodrich. *The Civil War in Kansas: Ten Years of Turmoil.*
    Charleston, SC: The History Press, 2012.

Carter, Robert A. Buffalo Bill Cody: *The Man Behind the Legend.* New York: John
    Wiley & Sons, 2000.

Castel, Albert. *Civil War Kansas: Reaping the Whirlwind.* Lawrence, KS: The
    University Press of Kansas, 1997.

The Civil War: A Visual History. London: Dorling Kindersley, 2011.

Cody, William F., *An Autobiography of Buffalo Bill.* Reprint of 1920 Farrar &
    Rinehart edition, Project Gutenberg, June 25, 2004 (#12740). www.gutenberg.
    org/files/12740/. Originally published 1920 in New York by the Cosmopolitan
    Book Corporation.

———., *The Life and Adventures of "Buffalo Bill" (1917)—The Final Edition
    of an Evolving Autobiography.* Archives of the West, the West Film Project.
    www.pbs.org/weta/thewest/resources/archives/seven/w67bbauto/w67bb0.htm.
    Originally published 1917 in Chicago by Stanton and Van Vliet.

———. *The Life of Hon. William F. Cody, Known as Buffalo Bill (1879).* Lincoln:
    University of Nebraska Press, 2011.

Davis, Kenneth S. *Kansas: A Bicentennial History.* New York: W. W. Norton,
    1976.

Friesen, Steve. *Buffalo Bill: Scout, Showman, Visionary.* Golden, CO: Fulcrum
    Publishing, 2010.

Gilmore, Donald L. *Civil War on the Missouri-Kansas Border.* Gretna, LA:
    Pelican Publishing Company, 2006.

Goodrich, Thomas. *Bloody Dawn: The Story of the Lawrence Massacre.* Kent,
    OH: The Kent State University Press, 1991.

Goodwin, Doris Kearns. *Team of Rivals: The Political Genius of Abraham
    Lincoln.* New York: Simon & Schuster, 2005.

Harrold, Stanley. *Border War: Fighting over Slavery before the Civil War.* Chapel
    Hill: University of North Carolina Press, 2010.

John Brown and Bleeding Kansas: Prelude to the Civil War. Lawrence, KS:
    Territorial Kansas Heritage Alliance, 2011.

Kirkman, Paul. *The Battle of Westport: Missouri's Great Confederate Raid.* Charleston, SC: The History Press, 2011.

Leonard, Elizabeth Jane, and Julia Cody Goodman. *Buffalo Bill: King of the Old West.* New York: Library Press, 1855.

Leslie, Edward E. *The Devil Knows How to Ride: The True Story of William Clarke Quantrill and His Confederate Raiders.* New York: Random House, 1996.

Neely, Jeremy. *The Border Between Them: Violence and Reconciliation on the Kansas-Missouri Line.* Columbia: The University of Missouri Press, 2007.

Nichols, Alice. *Bleeding Kansas.* New York: Oxford University Press, 1954.

Pickett, Calder M. *Voices of the Past.* Columbus, OH: Grid, 1977.

Russell, Don. *The Lives and Legends of Buffalo Bill.* Norman: University of Oklahoma Press, 1960.

Sell, Henry Blackman, and Victor Weybright. *Buffalo Bill and the Wild West.* Basin, WY: Big Horn Books, 1979.

Settle, Raymond W., and Mary Lund. *War Drums and Wagon Wheels: The Story of Russell, Majors and Waddell.* Lincoln: University of Nebraska Press, 2005.

Stratton, Joanna L. *Pioneer Women: Voices from the Kansas Frontier.* New York: Simon and Schuster, 1981.

Ward, Geoffrey C. *The West: An Illustrated History.* Boston: Little, Brown, 1996.

Warren, Louis S. *Buffalo Bill's America: William Cody and the Wild West Show.* New York: Vintage Books, 2005.

Wetmore, Helen Cody, *Last of the Great Scouts: The Life Story of William F. Cody.* Project Gutenberg, February 18, 2006. (#1248). www.gutenberg. org/files/1248/. Originally published 1899 by the Duluth Press Publishing Company in Duluth, Minnesota.

Yost, Nellie Snyder. Buffalo Bill: *His Family, Friends, Fame, Failures, and Fortunes.* Chicago: The Swallow Press, 1979.

"The Pony Express" by Todd Underwood. frontiertrails.com/oldwest/ponyexpress.htm

IMAGE CREDITS

Amon Carter Museum of American Art, Fort Worth, Texas: 132 (Charles M. Russell, *In Without Knocking*, 1909. Oil on canvas. 1961.201);

Buffalo Bill Center of the West, Cody, Wyoming, USA: x (Given in memory of William R. Coe and Mai Rogers Coe, 8.66), 2 (LBB.021), 6 (P.6.672), 8 (Gift of Winchester-Western Division, Olin Corporation, 25.70), 28 (LBB.019), 34 (LBB.040), 42 (LBB.042), 45 (LBB.043), 53 (Mary Jester Allen collection, 70.69) , 58 (26.77), 65 (LBB.045), 88 (BBatWWpg.020), 111 (LBB.096), 119 (LBB.113), 144 (Original Buffalo Bill Museum Collection, P.69.1575), 146 (Garlow Collection, P.69.2078), 162 (P.6.301), 164 (LBB.163), cover (right inset, colorized) and 165 (P.6.163), cover (bottom, colorized) and 167 (Gift of The Coe Foundation, 42.69), back cover (colorized) 172-173 (Original Buffalo Bill Museum Collection, Jennings, W.M., Photographer, P.69.54), 175 (Gift of the Coe Foundation, 1.69.74), 176 (P.69.88), 177 (Vincent Mercaldo Collection, P.71.809), 181 (Original Buffalo Bill Museum Collection, 1.69.442), 182 (BBatWWpg.169), 188 (P.69.898), 189 (David R. Phillips Collection, PN.47.4), 192 (Gift of D.F. Barry, P.69.2127), 205 (P.6.726), 208 (P.6.878);

Buffalo Bill Museum and Grave, Golden, Colorado: cover (left inset, colorized) 85, 185;

Kansas State Historical Society: cover (top, colorized), xiii (modern cities added for reference), 9, 18, 19, 21, 23, 26, 35, 36-37, 49, 55, 60, 61, 67, 68 (both images), 69, 74, 75, 76, 79, 80, 98, 99, 103, 105, 105, 107, 115, 121, 124, 130, 135, 137, 139, 142, 149, 156, 159, 193, 194, 195, 196, 197, 202;

Library of Congress: 14, 90, 148;

State Historical Society of Missouri: 128

INDEX

A

abolitionists, 34, 41, 49, 54,
    55 (photo), 67–70.
    See also Brown, John
African-American soldiers, 196–197
Alexis, Duke of Russia, 165–166
Anderson, "Bloody Bill," 135
architecture, 20
army
    enlistment in, 144, 147
    scout in, 148–153, 163
    spy for, 148, 149–151, 157
Atchison, 49

B

Bates, Sergeant, 182–183
Beecher, Henry Ward, 54, 55
    (photo), 68
"Beecher's Bibles," 54
Betsy (horse), 1–2
Bighorn Basin, 205
Billings, Horace, 27–29, 31
Billings, Sophia, 27
Black Jack, Battle of, 77
Bleeding Kansas, xiii, 70, 76, 82,
    160, 184
Border War, 195, 199–203
bread, 12–13, 27, 30, 52, 99, 157
Bridger, Jim, 107
Brown, Frederick, 80–81

Brown, Jason, 81
Brown, John
    death of, 193–194
    description of, 70–71, 193–194
    Harpers Ferry raid, 193
    Osawatomie battles by, 80–81
    in Pottawatomie Massacre, 75–77
    Underground Railroad
        participation by, 78
buffalo, 11, 26, 38, 100, 163, 164
    (photo), 170, 174, 179, 187
Buffalo Bill
    clothing worn by, xi, 165, 185
    (photo), 188
    creation of, 161–169
    image of, 165 (photo), 185 (photo),
    187–188
    novels about, 164, 166
    origin of name, 163
    play about, 166
*Buffalo Bill, the King of Border
    Men*, 164
Buffalo Bill Center of the West, 204
Buffalo Bill Dam, 191, 205
Buffalo Bill Museum, 204–205
Buffalo Bill Ranch State Historical
    Park, 204–205
buffalo hunts, 165–166, 177
Buffalo Soldier Monument, 201
buffalo soldiers, 162

Buntline, Ned, 163–164, 166
burial, 190
Burns, Mrs., 13
Burnt District, 199
Bushwhackers, 126, 131–135, 138, 140, 152, 158, 200

C

Carson, Kit, 108
cattle herding, 57–59, 58 (photo), 86–87, 90–92 , 90 (photo)
cattle ranch, 204
cavalry, 22, 102, 147
ceremonial war dances, 30–31, 177, 192
Cheyenne Indians, 107 (photo), 108, 130 (photo), 169
children, 162 (photo), 165, 189–190
Churchill, Lord and Lady Randolph, 180
Churchill, Winston, xii, 180
Church of Jesus Christ of Latter-Day Saints, 95
Civil War, xii–xiii
    deaths from, 199
    Kansas before and after, 196–198
    soldier in, 147, 155–160
    start of, 123, 200–201
    Wilson's Creek battle, 126, 157, 199
Cody, Arta, 162 (photo)
Cody, Billy/Bill
    accomplishments of, xii
    appearance of, xi
    as "Buffalo Bill." *See Buffalo Bill*

(Cody, Billy/Bill, cont.)
    childhood of, 6 (photo), 7–11
    as "Colonel," 180
    death of, 187
    employment of, 87–93, 95, 106, 129
    hunting skills of, 10
    photographs of, 6, 85, 165, 185
    upbringing of, 7–11
    in Wild West show. *See Wild West show*
Cody, Charles Whitney, 56–57, 160
Cody, Elijah, 4, 7, 13, 15–17, 19–20, 25, 27, 29, 30, 32, 42, 52, 57, 85, 87
    pro-slaver threats against, 53
    slave ownership by, 14, 16, 40
    trading store owned by, 35–36
Cody, Eliza, 8
Cody, Helen, 8, 47, 86, 89, 144
Cody, Irma, 190
Cody, Isaac, 2–5, 8, 11–16, 20, 22–25, 27–30, 32–35, 45 (photo), 64, 65, 70, 87–88, 94, 136, 140, 143, 201
    anti-slavery beliefs of, 14, 40–41, 43, 50
    death of, 85
    at Fort Leavenworth, 48
    free-state efforts by, 61–62
    as Free State Party legislator, 73
    in Ohio, 82, 84
    pneumonia in, 85
    pro-slavers threats against, 44–46, 50, 56, 62–63
    stabbing of, 41–43, 42 (photo)
    threats against, 44–46, 50, 56, 71

Cody, Joseph, 84

Cody, Julia, 2, 8, 16, 30, 36, 43–44,
    53, 82, 84–85, 93, 105–106, 132,
    143–144, 190

Cody, Kit Carson, 165

Cody, Louisa (Frederici), 161, 162
    (photo), 165–166, 168, 189–190

Cody, Martha, 8, 11, 94

Cody, Mary, 3, 8, 12, 20, 23, 25, 30,
    33, 37, 42–43, 45–47, 50–52,
    56–58, 83, 85, 89, 94–95, 106, 125,
    127–128
    Civil War and, 125
    death of, 143–145, 157–158
    free-state settlers welcomed by,
        62
    lawsuit against, 87–88
    marriage to Isaac Cody, 11
    photograph of, 144 (photo)
    slavery and, 14
    threats against, 82–84
    tuberculosis in, 86, 95, 106
    upbringing of, 10–11

Cody, Mary Hannah, 8

Cody, Ora Maude, 168

Cody, Sam, 1–3, 7, 8

Cody, Wyoming, 191, 204

"Cody Bloody Trail," 43

Colorado, 109, 116, 134

Comanche Indians, 108, 129

Conestoga wagons, 8, 24

Confederacy, 125, 157

Congressional Medal of Honor,
    xii, 167

conservation, 191, 205

cowboy hats, 180, 185 (photo)

cowgirls, xi, 177, 188 (photo),
    188–189

Crawford, Samuel J., 197

Custer, George Armstrong, 130
    (photo), 162, 169, 178–179

D

Danites, 101

Deadwood stagecoach, 174, 176
    (photo), 177, 179, 182

Douglass, Frederick, 194

drinking, 190

Dunn, Charles, 41–43, 51, 85

E

education, 11, 37, 62–63, 108–109

Eighth Kansas Infantry, 156 (photo)

Eldridge Hotel, 202

England, 179–183

Europe, 179–183, 208

Ewing, Thomas, 133

Exodusters, 198

F

ferries, 19 (photo), 20

Forrest, Nathan Bedford, 147–148,
    148 (photo), 150–151, 156, 195

Fort Bridger, 101–102, 103 (photo),
    104, 107

Fort Henry, 24

Fort Kearny, 89–92

Fort Laramie, 24, 103, 106–107, 110

Fort Larned, 129

Fort Leavenworth, 16–22, 21 (photo),

(Fort Leavenworth, cont.)
24, 28, 32–34, 40, 47, 48, 76, 88,
136, 141, 158, 160, 197, 201
Fort McPherson, 168
Fort Sumter, 194, 200–201
Frederici, Louisa. *See Cody, Louisa (Frederici)*
free-state efforts, 14–15, 34, 48–49,
54, 61–62, 76, 123
Free State Hotel, 67 (photo), 74–75,
140
Free State Party, 61, 69, 123
Frontier Army Museum, 201
frontiersman, 10, 95, 98, 155, 166

G
gateway to the West, 24
Geary, John White, 82
General Order Number 11, 199
Grasshopper Falls, 52, 56, 62–64, 71,
82, 84, 201
Greeley, Horace, 76
guerrillas, 126, 135, 147, 200

H
Harpers Ferry, 193
Harrington, Dave, 109, 112
Haskell Indian Nations University, 203
hay burning, 44
herders, 58–59, 90 (photo), 90–92, 99
(photo), 101–103
herding of cattle, 57–59, 58 (photo),
86–87, 90–92
Hickok, James Butler "Wild Bill,"
99–100, 102, 105 (photo),

(Hickok, James Butler "Wild Bill," cont.)
105–106, 117, 129, 157, 168, 195–
196, 201
horsemanship, 29
horse stealing, 117, 119 (photo),
127–128
horse thieves, 116, 119–121
hunting, 4, 10–11
Hurricane Creek, 156

I
Illinois, 34
Indians, 129–130.
See also Native Americans
attacks by, 91, 100, 116–117
battles against, 167
ceremonial war dances by, 30–31, 192
at Fort Laramie, 107
at Fort Leavenworth, 21
Kickapoo, 25, 26 (photo), 29–30
trading with, 29
Indian tribes.
See also Native Americans
list of, 108
Plains, 108, 178
Pony Express attacks by, 116–117
relocation to reservations, 4, 25, 192
Sioux, 110
Iowa, 1, 4, 5, 7, 8, 11, 34, 38, 204
Irma Hotel, 204, 205 (photo)
Irving, Henry, 180

J
James, Frank, 135, 199
James, Jesse, 135, 199

(Leavenworth, cont.)
57, 59, 73, 85, 87, 88, 92, 97, 98, 127, 143, 144, 161, 194, 201

Leavenworth Daily Times, 115 (photo)

LeClaire, Iowa, 7, 11, 204

Lecompton, 74, 202

Lee, Robert E., 193

Lenexa, 195

Lexington, 157

Lincoln, Abraham, 82, 123, 129, 194

Little Bighorn, Battle of the, 169, 178

London, 179, 180, 207

Lone Wolf, 207, 208 (photo)

Lookout Mountain, 190, 205

Loose Park, 203

Louisiana Street, 202–203

Lyons, Miss, 62, 163

M

mail, 114–122

Majors, Alexander, 87, 89, 95

Marmaduke, John, 160

Massachusetts Street, 138, 202 (photo)

McCracken Research Library to Advance the Study of the American West, 204–205

militias, 72–73, 80, 101, 132

Mine Creek, 159

Mississippi River, 125, 157

Missouri
after Civil War, 198–199
Burnt District, 199
Confederacy in, 125
description of, 4, 7, 34

(Missouri, cont.)
Kansas-Missouri border, xii, 66, 126, 133, 158
pro-slave settlers of, 49 (photo), 49–50

Missourians
Bushwhackers, 126, 131–135, 138, 140, 152, 158, 200
in Civil War, 198
horse stealing from, 127–128
militias of, 132
Osceola raid against, 126–127

Missouri River, xii, 4, 7, 18–20, 49

Mormons, 22, 24, 89, 94–104

Mormon Trail, 96, 107

Mound City, 160

Mountain Meadows, 96

Mount Oread, 67, 200, 202

N

Native Americans.
See also Indians; Indian Tribes; specific Indian tribe
Buffalo Bill's views on, 191–192
dress of, 25
in Wild West show, xii, 171, 172–173 (photo), 177–179, 192, 207–208, 208 (photo)

Nebraska, 15, 163, 166, 168, 171, 189, 204, 209

Nebraska National Guard, 181

Nebraska Territory, 89, 91

Neosho, 124–125

New England Emigrant Aid Company, 67

Jayhawkers, 126, 128, 131–132, 136, 149, 131–132, 195, 200
Jefferson City, 125
Jennison, "Doc," 149 (photo)
Jim Crow laws, 198
Johnson, Thomas, 59
John Wornall House, 203
Jones, Sheriff, 74–75

K

Kansas
  abolitionists in, 34
  African American settlers in, 198
  after Civil War, 196–198
  Bleeding, xiii, 70, 76, 82, 160, 184, 187, 201, 203
  free-state efforts in, 14–15, 34, 49, 54, 61–62, 76, 123
  Free State Party in, 61, 123
  guerrilla fighters from, 126
  Jayhawkers, 126, 128, 131–132, 195, 200
  John Brown's war in, 75–76
  John White Geary as governor of, 82
  map of, xiii
  militias in, 68, 71–72, 132
  move to, 4–5
  pro-slavery efforts in, 44–46, 50, 59–61, 60 (photo), 73–76
  slave escapes to, 124 (photo)
  squatters in, 33–34, 34 (photo)
  statehood for, 123–125
  terrain of, 23 (photo)
  towns in, 34

(Kansas, cont.)
  in Union, 123–125
  violence in, 74–79
  voting by Missourians in, 49 (photo), 50, 54
  Wilson Shannon as governor of, 71, 77
Kansas City, 133, 135, 158, 199, 203
Kansas-Missouri border, xii, 66, 126, 133, 158
Kansas-Nebraska Act, 15, 32
Kansas River, 19, 34, 67
Kansas Territory, 3, 4, 7, 25, 32, 34, 37, 43, 61, 124, 202
Kickapoo tribe, 25, 26 (photo), 29–30
Kiowa Indians, 108, 129
Ku Klux Klan, 195

L

Lakota Sioux Indians, 177, 178, 208 (photo)
Lane, Jim, 69 (photo), 70–71, 74, 82, 126, 136, 141, 194
Lawrence, 34, 50, 54, 61
  abolitionist leaders in, 68–69
  businesses in, 67
  founding of, 68
  militia in, 72–73
  modern-day, 202–203
  population of, 74
  Quantrill's raid, 134–142, 137 (photo), 139 (photo), 142 (photo), 196, 202 (photo)
Lawrence, Amos, 68
Leavenworth, 34, 35 (photo), 38, 49,

New York, 95, 166, 179, 180

New York Tribune, 76

O

Oakley, Annie, xi, 177, 183

Ohio, 10, 71, 82, 84, 135

Olathe, 136

Oregon Trail, 20, 97, 107

Osawatomie, 70, 77, 80–81

Osceola, 126–127, 136, 138

Oxford, 157

P

Pawnee Indians, 178, 208 (photo)

Pierce, Franklin, 32, 49, 72–73, 76–77, 82

Plains Indians, 108, 178

Platte River, 89, 91, 97

Plum Creek, 91

Plymouth Congregational Church, 67

pneumonia, 85, 207

polygamy, 95–96

Pony Express, xii, 114–123, 170, 177

Pottawatomie Creek, 75

Pottawatomie Massacre, 75–76

Powder River, 117

Price, Sterling, 157–160, 199

Prince of Wales, 180, 182

Prince (pony), 27–28, 28 (photo), 38, 50–51, 56, 63–64

pro-slavers

description of, 48–49

in Kansas, 44–46, 50, 59–61, 60 (photo), 73–76

(pro-slavers, cont.)

in Missouri, 49 (photo), 49–50

opposition to school by, 63

threats against Isaac Cody, 44–46, 50, 56, 62

Q

Quantrill, William Clarke

background on, 133–136, 196

Lawrence massacre by, 134–142, 137 (photo), 139 (photo), 142 (photo), 196, 202 (photo)

photograph of, 135 (photo)

R

Rain-in-the-Face, 110

Red Legs, 131, 134, 136, 195

Reeder, Andrew Horatio, 49

rifles, 8, 48, 54, 91, 100

Rively, Mr. M. P., 24, 35, 40, 42

Robinson, Charles, 68 (photo), 69, 71, 74, 126, 136, 138, 142, 194

Robinson, Sara, 68 (photo), 142, 202 (photo)

Rolla, 129

Roosevelt, Theodore, 191

Russell, Majors & Waddell, 24, 34, 87, 103, 114, 117, 122, 129

Russell, William, 38, 57, 89

S

Saint Joseph, 114

Saint Louis, 19, 35, 114, 158, 161–162

Salt Creek Valley

cabin in, 25, 28, 33

(Salt Creek Valley, cont.)
claim to land in, 32–33
description of, 201
life in, 23, 32–39
travelers through, 36–37 (photo)
Salt Lake City, 24, 29, 97, 100
Santa Fe Trail, 20, 59, 129
scarlet fever, 84–85
school, 25, 37, 62–63, 67, 95, 106, 108–109, 131, 135, 140
scout, xii, 9, 11, 38, 46, 62, 80, 117, 129, 131, 138, 148–153, 160–163, 165, 167–169, 195, 209
Scout's Rest Ranch, 204
Seventh Kansas Cavalry, 144, 147
Shannon, Wilson, 71, 77
sharpshooters, xii, 177–178
Shawnee, 136
Shawnee Indian Mission, 59
Sherman, William, 148, 161–162
Simpson, Lew, 98, 100–101
Sioux Indians, 107, 108, 110, 111, 178, 179, 207, 208
Sioux War, 169
Sitting Bull, 177–179, 192 (photo)
slavery, 12–16, 34
slaves. *See also* abolitionists; *pro-slavers*
description of, 4
escape of, to Kansas, 124 (photo)
illustration of, 14 (photo)
John Brown's opposition to, 70
in Missouri, 34
Smith, Andrew Jackson, 148, 151, 152–154, 156

Smith, Joseph, 95–96
Smith, Lott, 101–102
soldier in Civil War, 155–160
sports, 30, 200
Springfield, 126, 129
spy, 147, 149–151, 157
squatters, 33–34, 34 (photo)
SS *Nebraska*, 179
steamboats, 17–18, 18 (photo), 114, 147, 157
storytelling, 164, 168
Stowe, Harriet Beecher, 54
Stranger Creek, 63
supply trains, 24, 106

T
telegraph, 88, 121, 122
Tennessee, 147–149, 195
Tennessee Street, 202–203
Topeka Constitution, 61, 61 (photo)
trading store, 35–36
trappers, 26–28
Treaty of Lawrence, 72
tuberculosis, 86, 95, 106
Tubman, Harriet, 194
Tuff, Bill, 131
Tupelo, 156
Turk (dog), 8, 10, 17, 38, 46, 51–52, 104
Twain, Mark, xii, 178
typhoid fever, 160

U
Uncle Tom's Cabin (Stowe), 54
Underground Railroad, 34, 70, 78, 136, 194

Union army. *See army*
University of Kansas, 200, 202
University of Missouri, 200
Utah, 22, 89, 95–97

V

Valley Falls, 201
Valley of the Great Salt Lake, 96–97
Victoria, Queen of England, xii, 179,
181–183, 208

W

wagons
Conestoga, 8, 24
driving of, 98–100
wagon trains, 9, 19, 20, 29, 38, 89,
102–103, 108–109, 134, 143
Weston, 4, 7, 10, 13, 15, 20, 25, 27, 28,
30, 32, 35, 36, 42, 49, 52, 57, 85
Westport
Battle of, 158, 159 (photo), 199,
203
description of, 59, 127, 203
white bread, 12–13
Wild Bill Hickok. *See Hickok, James
Butler "Wild Bill"*
Wilde, Oscar, 180
Wild West show
advertising of, 174, 175 (photo)
animals in, 171, 174, 179
Annie Oakley in, xi, 177, 183
Buffalo Bill's entrance into, 182.
See also Buffalo Bill
buffalo hunts in, 177
cast of, xi–xii, 172 (photo), 174, 179

(Wild West show, cont.)
cowgirls in, xi, 177, 188 (photo),
188–189
creation of, 163–166, 168–184
Deadwood stagecoach in, 174,
176 (photo), 177, 179, 182
elements of, 175, 177
in Europe, 179–183, 208
first performances of, 171
members of, 172–173 (photo)
Native Americans in, xii, 171,
172–173 (photo), 177–179,
192, 207–208, 208 (photo)
payment of members of, 179, 188
Plains Indians in, 178
posters for, 174, 175 (photo), 180,
181 (photo)
publicizing of, 171, 174
sharpshooters in, xi, 177–178
Wilson's Creek, 126, 157, 199
Wisconsin, 25
women, 188–190
Woodson, Daniel, 77
Wornall Road, 203
Wyoming, 24, 101, 103, 106,
116–117, 191, 204, 209

Y

Yellow Hair, 169
Yellowstone National Park, 191
Young, Brigham, 96–97, 101
Younger, Cole, 135, 199

ANDREA WARREN combines her love of history and story with her passion for children and education in her award-winning nonfiction books. Her many honors include the *Boston Globe-Horn Book* Award for Nonfiction, the Robert F. Sibert Honor Award for Most Distinguished Informational Book for Children, and the Orbis Pictus Award for Outstanding Nonfiction for Children. Reviewers and readers have called her books "riveting," meticulously researched," and a "top flight example of historical storytelling."

Warren lives in eastern Kansas, where much of this book is set. For more information about her books please visit AndreaWarren.com.